WOMAN:
HER INTUITION
FOR OTHERNESS

The Path of Christian Meditation

੨൦

Eileen P. O'Hea, C.S.J.

੨൦

The Benedictine Priory

Montreal

In gratitude to all who have
loved me and companioned me
along the way . . .
and
with appreciation to all, known and
unknown, who love and strive to
have our world find the truth
of itself in a model of universal
love and friendship.

Excerpts from *The Jerusalem Bible* copyright © 1966 by
Darton, Longman & Todd, Ltd. and Doubleday, a division
of Bantam, Doubleday, Dell Publishing Group, Inc. Reprinted
by permission of Darton, Longman & Todd, Ltd. and Bantam,
Doubleday, Dell Publishing Group, Inc.

The Canticle of Mary from *The New Companion to the Breviary*,
copyright © 1988 by the Carmelites of Indianapolis.
Reprinted by permission of the Carmelites of Indianapolis.

ISBN 0-919815-22-7
Manufactured in the United States of America

Contents

III
REFLECTIONS FOR
THE JOURNEY
Mantra Prayer

Inside Forgiveness

Foreword

One of the great explanatory symbols of the experience of meditation is the journey. It is a process, an adventure, a constant leaving and arriving.

Eileen O'Hea has shared with us in this book her insight into the centrality of this journey from ourselves to the Divine Other. Central to every human life that is moving into fuller consciousness, the journey is central to the Christian conception of life as a following of the Way.

Eileen's ministry and mission is a continuously evolving one of healing and inspiration. As therapist or spiritual guide, she speaks in words or silence from the same journey out of which she wrote this book.

The journey, as she witnesses, is one to wholeness and peace, to an integration of the female and male dimensions of God and all creatures. Out of this integration flows the love that reveals the person we encounter on this journey: the encounter that is the journey.

LAURENCE FREEMAN, O.S.B.

Church

in Christ
at-oned
mother
daughter
sister
father
brother
son
each known
separateness
atoned

in Christ
no-one
each in each
father in mother
daughter in brother
sister in son
distinctions
none

in Christ
oned
one in the All
who is
and who is
All
in all

Introduction

Dear Companion Along the Way,

Christian meditation is a way of prayer that leads us to the full realization of our identity. It is a way to union and unity with all and a way to that place where differences no longer separate; a place where what is peculiarly masculine or feminine is neither submerged, discounted, nor forgotten; a place where integrity is known.

Christian meditation is the way that can bring us to the full realization of our womanhood and manhood because it leads us to the truth of our being. The truth of our being is that we are in relationship with Divine Being; we are in Love.

We intuit this truth at moments of our life, but the truth quickly escapes us. Christian meditation is a path to that experience of knowing ourselves as loved and in relationship with Divine Otherness.

Woman: Her Intuition for Otherness reflects through persons and themes the desire and struggle to pursue and respond to the most intimate of relationships, namely, our relationship with the Divine Other.

This book is an invitation into that experience. It is a book written for both women and men that focuses on woman and themes involving relationship. Because it is the product of a human endeavor, it is culture bound.

Woman is named and extolled because she reflects and embodies in our age what is essential to the reign of God in our world: relationship to others—the Other and all others. This intuition for otherness, expressed by woman, mirrors the Reality that makes it possible, namely, identity realized in the presence of Divine Love.

The spiritual and psychological dynamics that are part of our journey into the experience of Oneness are addressed in the beginning chapters of this book. It is important to note that in the language of psychology, the term *ego* is used to describe the dynamics of human personality, but in this book we will use the word *ego* to denote the *false* perception of self. The second section focuses on the specifics involved in the practice of Christian meditation as the way to this Oneness and the truth of our identity. The last section is meant to lead the journeyer into the daily practice of Christian meditation via a series of reflections on Scripture texts involving women or themes considered feminine.

Like the practice of Christian meditation itself, the words found on these pages are meant to lead the journeyer into a practice of prayer that is beyond words. The words within this book arise from my own journey, those things I needed explained or identified before I could be sure it was "safe" to go beyond words.

More than ten years ago, I began listening to the taped conferences of John Main, OSB. His message seemed to speak directly to my heart, moving me to respond in prayer through the practice of Christian meditation.

The message of John Main made sense to me, and I intuitively recognized the prayer of Christian meditation as a way of truth. I have tried to meditate twice daily since that time and throughout the years have felt deeply connected to John Main and his teachings. Both for him and his companion and dear friend, Laurence Freeman, OSB, I am so very grateful. They have recovered from the rich heritage of Church tradition the mantra as a way of contemplative prayer. For me and for thousands of others throughout the world, this teaching presents a pathway to the realization of full consciousness.

God's reign, I believe, is synonymous with human identity realized completely. This happens as our awareness widens and deepens, becomes awake to all those parts of ourselves that have been submerged. Both women and men have repressed, denied, discounted, or misinterpreted the feminine that is in each of us because it represents the presence of otherness that cannot be controlled or manipulated and is, therefore, feared.

As woman pursues her intuition for otherness, she claims the lost or submerged elements of the feminine within her. In so doing she expands her consciousness and breaks through the defensive structures that keep her from realizing full being in and with Divine Love. I know that it is only the hovering presence of Lady Wisdom that can elicit a response of the heart through the print found on these pages. Without her inspiration, the words of these pages join the already overflowing information banks in each of us. With the gift of her spirit, the words can be the medium that empowers us to take the next step of our journey toward Oneness.

❧ . . . She is a breath of the power of God, . . . Although alone, she can do all; herself unchanging, she makes all things new. In each generation she passes into holy souls, she makes them friends of God and prophets (Wisdom 7:25, 27–28). ❧

As a student and teacher of the practice of Christian meditation for the last ten years, I now know this prayer form is not only safe but also essential. It is essential to my own well-being and search for integrity and essential, I believe, for our world if we are to join with each other and realize and share our sisterhood and brotherhood.

And so, I welcome you, dear companion along the way, to share an experience of relationship that will never fail you, into an experience of love that exceeds what can be imagined, into the wordless experience of knowing.

With affection,
Eileen

I

THE SPIRITUAL JOURNEY: FAITH AND RELATIONSHIP

Discernment

Desperately
flaying the darkness
I try to grasp
that place or One
that beckons
me to come

Eyes blinded
ears deaf
I search the blackness
and yearn
to hear
my name
spoken
the darkness
broken

Encircled in my chaos
(chosen so deliberately)
I beg: pity, pity, pity
that your eagle wing
would swoop me past
the boundaries of myself

and drop me into that abyss
which
I have peripheried so well
        (my hell)
those depths of being
that I fear
that I dare

lift me then
from this self
I beg
and wing
my way to where
you are

Vagrant of all
but my desire
(that prayer of wordless sound)
I long for that place of your embrace
where
enveloped in you
I am forever lost
and forever found.

Otherness

The need to love and be loved, to be in relationship with someone is essential to the experience of being human. It is our desire to be known that brings us into relationship with others, since it is only here that our sense of self can emerge and develop. Without others, the self remains obscure, hidden, and unknown.

Both history and literature document the capacity women have for deep and intimate relationships with men and with other women. The deep level of sharing and love that is exchanged in women's relationships is not usually reflected in relationships between males, even though men often desire it. Both women and men share the need for intimate love, but women seem to have developed this capacity for relationships of love and friendship far more than most men.

Our twentieth century is witness to the individuation process occurring in the evolution of woman. This process incorporates the characteristics of self-individuation. It is an experience connected with knowing; we know because we are known. Sometimes the anonymity we are unconsciously experiencing is shocked into awareness, perhaps by someone recognizing us or calling us by name. Most frequently the unveiling of our anonymity is gradual and subtle and consists of multiple incidents such as the one that follows.

Karen, age eight, loved root beer sodas. Whenever she gathered the money she needed for one, she would stop at the local ice cream store. One day, after she had settled herself on the high stool at the counter, the waiter approached and asked, "What will you have today, young lady, a root beer soda?" Karen recounts this story, remembering the shock she experienced because someone outside herself recognized her and realized her existence.

Carl Jung's story of his individuation at age eleven is more dramatic and immediate. It happened as he walked to school one day. When he relates this incident, he remembers it as an experience of walking out of a heavy mist. His telling of this story indicates that he experienced life differently after this event, as though he had been awakened from a dream.

The individuation process that women are going through today is significant to both women and men because in it a deeper level of truth and reality is being experienced in human life. Women today are calling one another from a state of anonymity to one of realization of their own identity and inherent worth, one no longer confined to or dependent upon the perceptions of male cultural patterning or bias.

In rediscovering her identity, woman penetrates and reflects the mystery of human life and its ultimate destiny. In walking out of the mist of cultural patterning and a system of patriarchy often perpetuated by both women and men, woman is emerging and realizing a sense of self that is separate from but always in relationship to others. As she becomes more aware of the truth of her identity, so too does she deepen and expand her capacity for relationships of love and friendship. This is possible because all human identity exists in and in relationship to Divine Being.

Woman's intuition for otherness, her desire to be present to and known by others, reflects and incarnates the deepest of mystical truths, namely that human intuition moves us to use our freedom to entrust ourselves to the Divine Other. The deepest reality of human life is that we are in relationship with the Divine Other and that it is here that we experience ourselves as known, our identities realized fully. Human relationships of true intimacy and love are veiled participations in the reality of Divine Love present in human life.

Woman's developed gift for entering into relationships of intimacy and love is a paradigm for the modern world of a way of being with others that is foundational to human experience and, therefore, essential to God's reign in our world.

Commitment in Relationship

Woman has valued relationships of true love and friendship through the centuries because she has found in them a source of happiness as well as a means to her own self-actualization. Woman is cognizant of the fact, therefore, that commitment to another in love and friendship comes about only after a process of discovery has been entered into. This process requires a willingness to be known by the other and a desire to spend time with the other to allow that person to become known to us. Woman knows that the commitment stage of relationship can be arrived at only when there is a willingness to be open to the phases of relationship that precede it.

As a paradigm for human life, Jesus lived a life for and in the Divine Other, a life grounded in relationships of true love and friendship. In Jesus, God's self is expressed and made known to humanity. Jesus is God's Word spoken into human history. In Jesus, the intimate relationship of love that exists between God and human persons is realized.

Self-communication is essential to human relationships of true love and intimacy. When we feel it is safe to do so, we give the other the gift of sharing our very selves. Sharing with another what we know about ourselves—our fears, our ideas about life and love, our dreams, our struggles, and our awareness of the presence of God in our life—brings that other person as well as us into a greater conscious awareness of our own lived reality. In becoming known to another, we also become better known to ourselves.

Relationships of true love and friendship share in the divine act of redeeming us from the bondage of egocentricity, thereby helping us to become aware of how we are using our freedom. Human relationships have the potential of helping us to realize the choices we are making that are keeping us from turning completely toward the Divine Other.

Women have intuited that self-discovery and self-revelation are part of the process that leads to the joy and happiness found in relationships of committed love. Women also know that human relationships involve a process through which ideas about love must be adjusted and purified. Because women have valued and cherished friendship, they have willingly persevered through that process.

The process of friendship seems to take us through three distinct stages. Frequently, what we discover in our attempts to love another is that under the guise of "love," we engage the other to satisfy the needs of our own ego. The human condition of feeling incomplete causes us to look to others to fill in what we feel is lacking within ourselves. We enter into relationships because they seem to offer us opportunities to be connected with others who will assuage our emptiness. Subtly or overtly, in the first stage of relationship, we look to the other to satisfy ourselves. We find the other attractive and see in that person all that is good. In this first stage of relationship, the attraction stage, our ontological anxiety (our unrealized desire for oneness with Divine Being) feels relieved by our finding "oneness" with another who seems able to complete us. The other with whom we are relating fills in, as it were, the lacks we are experiencing in ourselves. That person affirms us.

The attraction stage of relationship is very consuming. We are not only relieved of our anxiety but also distracted from our emptiness, guilt, and feelings of inferiority. All too soon, however, we begin to recognize that the other cannot complete us or meet demands well enough or often enough, and we realize that our expectations of the relationship will not be fulfilled. For some this will mean terminating the relationship and taking up the search for fulfillment in another relationship. This shifting of emotional investment from one relationship to another highlights the egocentricity involved in relating. When the other is no longer useful to us, that person is no longer valued. In other words, since the other has not produced the desired effect for us, the relationship no longer seems worth our time and energy. The attraction is gone.

For those who view relationship from a female system, there can be a willingness to recognize the differences and failed expectations that emerge and to continue in the relationship in the acknowledgment stage. In this stage we recognize that we wanted the other to be in our own image and likeness. We wanted that person to give us a sense of identity and self-worth. We wanted the other to make us good or holy. When the other fails us in this project that we have devised, we are angry and disappointed.

For those of us who do not shift our energies to a new relationship or project (such as overinvolvement with work), the relationship becomes the opportunity for identifying our own self-preoccupation and egocentricity. At this stage of relationship, we can discover that the demands we are making of the other underscore a subliminal belief that we are indeed autonomous and have no need of God, that we are able to complete ourselves through others.

The second stage of relationship can be the period in which we learn that trying to use or possess the other for our own sake results in misery and dissatisfaction. It is in this stage that we begin to glimpse true love. We realize it is other-centered and not self-centered. The self-realization that is made possible through relationship allows those things that keep us bound in egocentricity to surface to consciousness. Relationships can be the place where we once again acknowledge that we are dependent on Divine Love to rescue us from the bondage of egocentricity.

Much of the pain involved in relationships is the result of the self-definition we experience when others refuse our demands. We, consequently, feel attacked, hurt, or betrayed by them because they have not loved us the way they "should" or the way we want them to. This is not to say that others do not act hurtfully or unjustly toward us. They do, and we act unjustly toward them as long as we identify with our egos. The ego is the experience of dismembering or fragmentation. When we are re-membered instead to a place of truth—our true selves—we know in that place of identity unsurpassable love, love that is complete and cannot be diminished. Human relationships are the opportunities that call us back, that re-member us to the truth of our identity.

Our relationship with another also provides us with a companion who will continue to love us even when we experience ourselves (wrongly) as unlovable. Although our attempts at love may reveal how distorted and selfish our ideas about love are, these attempts to love, however imperfect, are the paths that lead to the discovery of true love. Relationships of true love and friendship are the meeting places of those willing to discover true love by being companions to each other in the struggle toward true identity. As such, relationships of true love and friendship are the quintessential gift of human life.

The third stage, the commitment stage of relationship, is reached when differences are acknowledged and valued, and the other is loved for herself or himself. Differences in the other are no longer seen as obstacles to the relationship or as places of separation. The commitment stage is the joining of individuals in the process of true love and friendship in which the other is loved for his or her own sake. And because the other is perceived as good and lovable, we are willing to trust that person with the gift of ourselves. Our conversations with the other are the holy ground where we communicate ourselves and are received in love. Our time together is the sacred space in which realized love enables us to come more deeply into truth. Relationships of true love and friendship are undisputed gifts because they are the place of God's healing, redeeming, and reconciling activity.

It is this gift for true love and friendship, which woman has incorporated into her life, that has enabled in our time the bonding of women throughout our world. And it is this gift that woman holds before human consciousness as the way to the experience of love, justice, and peace in our world.

Entrusting Oneself
to the
Divine Other

Every decision seems to have at least two moments—the moment of the decision itself and the moment of deciding again after some time has been spent living into the initial decision. The second moment can be viewed as the moment of mature decision making because the commitment made at the second moment can be relied upon. It springs from decisions that incorporate the experiences of pain and struggle, happiness or satisfaction that are implicit to decision-making processes and commitment.

Entrusting ourselves to the Divine Other is a decision of the second moment in our faith histories. Such a decision cannot be made until we have struggled for years, perhaps a lifetime, with our own egocentricity. We can't truly experience ourselves (the true self) until we are freed from the bondage of our egos—from its illusions, fears, and misperceptions about our relationship to the Divine Other.

There is an unyielding intuition in us to experience love and to share love. Our relationships of love and friendship are always the enactment of this innate desire to join with others. We want to reach out and be connected to others in a love that is mutual, pure, and unselfish—a love that loves others for their own sakes, a love that does not use others as a means to our own fulfillment, a love that rejoices in the identity of others and encourages their growth.

There is no experience more wonderful than knowing we are loved. There is nothing so prized as the mutual love extended in friendship, and there is no human experience that touches divinity more than relationships of love. Human relationships of love and friendship are the cherished gifts of those who are awake to their intuition for otherness. Such relationships are the place where we know untold joy and ecstasy, and they are the place where we can experience the deepest pain and hurt. Although it is true that only through loving relationships can we learn what love really is, it is also true that our attempts to love reveal how little we know of true love and how incapable most of us are of loving unselfishly.

All of our relationships of love and friendship are the expression of our deepest desire to know and be known by another. They are also an opportunity to discover the dynamics of our ego, and this is projected into our relationships.

For the awakened heart, relationships of love and friendship cannot be separated from the source of their life, which is Divine Love. In our relationships, we glimpse the truth of love, its meaning, its depth, and its foreverness. In these glimpses of love, we recognize an experience that transcends our own finitude. It is an experience that alerts us to the limitlessness and unsurpassable nature of love, that reveals our destiny to be found and known in love.

Entrusting ourselves completely to the Divine Other is an intuition in us journeyers that begins to surface into conscious awareness because of these experiences of recognizing Love. However, although we begin to desire to entrust ourselves to the Divine Other, we also resist and fear the surrender because we wrongly associate it with a loss of identity, the obliteration of personal uniqueness, or the submission of personhood.

Until the layers of our ego-centered self are penetrated by love, we will entrench ourselves behind its walls. Much, if not all, of the pain and struggle involved in human relationships is the result of our fear and mistrust of love. We may fear intimacy with another because our emotional patterning has taught us, incorrectly, that love means fusing into another and, consequently, losing our identity. We may mistrust "love" either because we have experienced it as the projection of our own egocentricity demanding fulfillment and completion by using others, or because we have been the receivers of this kind of "love." Much of the anxiety involved in our attempts to love concerns learning when it is safe to be vulnerable to another, namely, when we can remove the masks of our defenses. Those who engage in intimate relationship with others risk rejection by exposing their very selves in the process of becoming known to another. Because we need to love and be loved, we look to human relationships of love to confirm the truth that we do not yet fully realize—namely, that we are lovable. When we experience ourselves as loved by others who cherish and value us simply for our own being, our intuition of the existence of a true self, a self that is lovable and inherently good, is confirmed and deepened. It is love that frees us from the fear that keeps us hiding behind the walls of our egocentricity, claiming it as the reality of our identity, making us afraid that our discovery will mean rejection and annihilation. It is love that calls us out of the bondage of our human conditioning into an experience of Othercenteredness where the true self is realized.

We perceive entrusting ourselves to the Divine Other as a risk that threatens us because we bring to this experience our own personal histories of love and relationship. We, therefore, project onto the Divine Other our limited experience of love. Because in relationship we have felt diminished or have diminished the personhood of others, we fear trusting ourselves to the Other; because we have dominated and controlled others, or they us, we fear the loss of self that was our experience; and because we experience ourselves as finite and limited, we resist or refuse the belief that there can be an experience that is not limited like our own.

For centuries, women's role in their relationship with men has been to act as the complement of the male ego. The loss of identity or the submerging of individuality for the sake of the male became the accepted position of women in relationships with men. It is not difficult to understand how woman might associate any idea of surrendering or entrusting herself to the Other with centuries of emotional history in which woman was seen as an object to be used by men for their fulfillment and aggrandizement. Most cultures throughout the world, as well as political and religious systems, propagated these beliefs and perpetuated the idea that since woman was inferior to man, she was not meant to share equal rights with men. As a result, many women themselves became blinded to their intrinsic worth and capabilities; they identified with the perceptions of male-dominated societies. It is no wonder, then, that today women throughout the nations of our world are so vigilant about issues of identity and equality.

Woman, as she approaches the twenty-first century, is asserting herself in our world, no longer willing to have her intuition for otherness lead to relationships that associate inequality, domination, control, or the sacrificing of identity with the true meaning of love and friendship.

Woman knows that the restructuring of our world through the model of relationships of true love and friendship is not only necessary but possible. She knows it is necessary because she recognizes that the systemic evil in our world is the result of collective egos projecting onto the world scene the same themes of inequality, domination, and control that have been part of her own experience; and woman knows that a model of universal love and friendship is possible because that, too, has been her experience. Women's intuition for otherness has survived the tragedy of male domination and oppression because it has been realized in relationships of love and friendship with other women and with men who have recognized the lack of truth and justice implicit in models of relating that do not express the experience of mutuality and equality.

For men who continue to identify their maleness with perpetuating themes of domination, power, and control, the invitation to entrust oneself in relationship to the Divine Other will be threatening. Both men and women, therefore, bring to their relationship with the Divine Other the accumulated joys and fears of their histories in relationship.

The in-breaking of Divine Love on human consciousness, however, is continually at work, drawing us from our ego world, its fears and misperceptions, into Truth and Love. Relationships of true love and friendship reflect this in-breaking of Divine Presence in human life and provide the opportunity for the self to realize its true identity.

As we journeyers become more conscious of the experience of love in our lives, we begin to recognize in this draw of Divine Love the invitation to move more deeply and completely toward it. Frequently, we experience this call to a faith decision of the second moment as the feeling that we are on the edge of a precipice and required to make a leap of faith; or we feel that we are being called to cross some boundary that will take us into the unknown. Hesitation, caused by the fear that overshadows our desire to respond wholeheartedly, seems to be our predominant experience as we travel along the way. Some remain on the periphery of this imagined edge for months or years.

Again, it is only the experience of love that can free us from our fear. That is why it is necessary that at such times we not give way to discouragement and turn away from the path of pure love because we feel our response to love is inadequate.

A spiritual guide can be most helpful at this significant moment in our faith histories. Such a person will encourage us to recognize that our fears are unfounded, that a conscious decision to move toward the Divine Other will in no way hurt or diminish us but will be an experience of new and greater life. A spiritual guide will urge us to be patient with ourselves as we experience our own limits and poverty, and to trust in the abundance and graciousness of Divine Love.

When decisions of the second moment of faith are made, that is, when the self decides to use its freedom to turn from egocentricity to Divine Otherness, no change is immediately apparent. Years of social and emotional patterning seem to continue in much the same way as they did before our decision. The struggle to be free of ego-centeredness—with its fears, its misperceptions of reality, and its desire to control us—continues. However, since Divine Love is dependent on the conscious decisions of women and men to accept it, our yes to this second moment of faith allows Divine Love to completely enter into us and thereby effect the mutual exchange of Divine Love and our love. This immersion into True Love eventually causes us to experience all of life differently. We begin to see with the eyes of faith. The reality of being known in the love that is exchanged with the Divine Other is a relationship that we experience as endless and expanding—one that knows no threat of abandonment, diminishment, or rejection. It is a relationship that exceeds anything that we can imagine or have previously known about the depth and beauty of love. It is an experience of loving that incorporates all our human relationships of love and friendship and brings each to full realization in us. In this relationship of love we feel safe, we feel at home, and we feel found in the truth of our identity.

So inexpressible is the wonder of this love that our hearts are moved to the full realization of this encounter in an experience that takes us beyond words, beyond silence, beyond knowing.

God's Reign: A Universal Model
of Relationships
of True Love and Friendship

Entrusting oneself to the Divine Other is a movement of the human heart away from egocentricity toward the draw of divine love. This movement is essential to God's reign in our world.

The evil that is so much a part of our world is the result of egocentricity. The inappropriate use of human freedom, self-preoccupation, and the preservation of our own lives over and against the lives of others through domination, control, violence, or the misuse of power have resulted in the lack of justice and peace in our world. Unless our human hearts are converted, entrusting themselves to the Divine Other, political, social, and economic restructuring will result only in collective egoism that finds new methods to perpetuate the same evil.

Expressions such as "global village" and "human family" have surfaced into the consciousness of women and men of the twentieth century to describe a new understanding of our world and our connection to each other. When the human heart is not blinded by egocentricity, it recognizes the call to unity that it intuits as the truth of human existence.

Woman is calling out to our modern world, inviting it and pleading with it to restructure itself on the model of human relationships of love and friendship. Her instinct is the instinct held in the heart of all women and men and can only be realized when it is no longer obscured by egoism. Woman finds in the relationships of true love and friendship that exist between individuals a paradigm for the relationship possible between groups of people and nations throughout our world. Today, women who present true love and friendship as the means of restructuring our world are reflecting in our age the gospel values and the reality expressed in the life, death, and resurrection of Jesus.

In Jesus, we see realized what is possible for human life. The gospel describes the love relationship of God with women and men and portrays through Jesus a model for human life, a way of friendship and love.

Since we can trace the systemic evil in our world to collective egoism, we can reason that a world of justice, peace, and love is only possible when our world structures are not the result of this projected egoism. Another dimension of the human person, one in harmony with its ultimate destiny, must be awakened and realized for this new happening. When this true self emerges out of the bondage of egoism, its realized identity will be found in loving relationship with the Other and all others. The peace, love, wholeness, and integrity that are all indigenous to this self will become the new reality of groups and nations who people our world.

Discovering that it is egoism that keeps human beings from experiencing the oneness with God and others that they long for, we question why human persons seem so heavily invested in egoism and we try to find ways to be free of it.

To be human is to be constantly involved in deciding how to use our freedom. We choose to move toward our own egos, thereby disassociating ourselves from the awareness of the Divine Draw, or, we turn from egocentricity and move more deeply into our relationship with the Other, and consequently others.

Jesus is "The Way" for Christians because in becoming a human person he expresses for humanity its true identity, which is a self completely turned toward and disposed to the Divine Other. As the expression of God in human history, Jesus never denied his creatureliness, which of its nature implies suffering and death. To be a creature means we, too, must accept death as intrinsic to life. To deny and resist death as part of life results in sin. The refusal to accept creaturehood and limits is a decision to turn inward rather than toward the Divine Other; this turning inward creates a world of false perceptions, a world of no death and therefore no limits.

Since death is part of creaturehood, the denial of death results in a belief that we are autonomous and not dependent on anything outside ourselves. Since the beginning of time, the God who created us intended us to reach full union in Divine Love and thereby achieve our own human fullness through the experiences of our creaturehood. So when death is denied or avoided, sin results. We live lives that are not other-centered but ego-centered.

It is the fear of death that keeps us from making the decision that will lead us into the realization of our full personhood in the Other. It is the decision of the ego to choose the safety and comfort of what is known, no matter how miserable or dis-eased, that is the bondage from which God in Jesus rescues us—our fear of death. Jesus' readiness to be like woman and man teaches us that he reached the full realization of himself in God in the death/resurrection mystery, and so do we. He teaches us that the spirit present in his life and death is present in us, and that in and with that Spirit, death is entered into and passed through.

Since all the children share the same blood and flesh, he [Jesus] too shared equally in it, so that by death he could take away all the power of the devil who had power over death, and set free all those who had been held in slavery all their lives by the fear of death (Hebrews 2:14–15).

As God's expression of human life, Jesus is for humanity the visible witness of the continuance of new life when death is entered into. Our final death threatens us with extinction and thereby fills us with a terror so great that it represses and denies death as a part of life. To be a creature means we must accept death as intrinsic to life. This refers to our final death or the cessation of life as we know it and also the continual death experience implicit in our life-long struggle to let go of—or die to—egocentricity.

Death is intrinsic to life. Solutions for peace—in the world, among families or groups, or within individuals—must include the acknowledgment of dying to egocentricity as inherent to peace. Relationships of true love and friendship always contain the dying process.

Denial and avoidance of death perpetuates sinful structures. The very fact that we do not want thoughts of death to enter our conversations, or that we feel our spirits dampened when the desires of our hearts for peace, justice, and love are linked with the death mystery, underscores the denial of death implicit in our makeup. In other words, in our individual lives and relationships, as well as in our concerns for a better world, we want new life, but somehow we still hold fast to a belief that we can experience new life without entering into the death mystery. This denial of death, therefore, is a denial of our creaturehood and represents our identification with egocentricity. The full realization of our identity cannot come about without our acceptance of the death mystery. The truth of our identity is that we were meant to live in loving relationship with the Other and all others. The death mystery as part of life is therefore part of the deepening experience of relationships of love and friendship. We are constantly called to use our freedom to turn completely toward the Divine Other, which means a dying to our ego selves.

God's reign in our world, therefore, is rooted in the conversion of the human heart. Conversion of the human heart concerns the use of human freedom, namely, the decision to turn away from egocentricity toward the draw of Divine Love. Intrinsic to this process is a willingness to enter into the death that is part of it, in faith. What enables us to enter into death and break through our fear is love realized in us. God's self-communication in Jesus is the visible manifestation of the love relationship that exists between God and humanity. Jesus teaches us that the same Spirit present in him is present in us, and that in and with that Spirit we can face into our final death and the many deaths required before we are freed of egocentricity. Like Jesus, we will find that when death is entered into in faith, we will experience new life.

The reign of God is the reign of love in human hearts. It is human personhood realizing full being and extending itself in love and friendship to others as it realizes itself in a relationship of intimate love in the Divine Other. It is the experience of the true self.

Modernity can be fooled into thinking that death is not being denied in our age because human consciousness holds within it the possibility of momentary and massive annihilation brought about by the ingenuity and technology of nations of our world. This threat of annihilation and massive death has brought world leaders together in the hope of finding ways that will prevent one group from destroying another. Agreements are negotiated that restrain and control humanity's destructive tendency to preserve one group's life over—and against—the lives of others. Consequently, we live in an atmosphere that keeps us vigilant and threatened, unsure of others' commitment to peace and mistrustful of them. What remains unaddressed, however, is the denial of death that underlies the engagements of peoples and nations in death-dealing behaviors, namely violence, control, and domination. What is ignored is the potential of human life to use its freedom to turn away from these destructive tendencies and transcend ego-centricity by entering into the death mystery. This conversion of the human heart is foundational to a world of true peace and justice for all women and men.

Thankfully, we humans have not been left stranded on our planet earth, and thankfully, we can make a choice other than egocentricity. The in-breaking of Divine Presence upon human consciousness is continually happening and inviting us to turn from our choice of an ego-centered world to a deeper reality—our true selves.

Woman, as she approaches the twenty-first century, reclaims her true identity and unearths for all people their potential to know themselves in love. Since the death mystery is part of human life, the full realization of our identity cannot come about unless we live into it in faith. Because the truth of our identity is realized in relationships of true love and friendship that call us beyond our ego selves, the death that is implicit in that call must therefore be seen as essential to the deepening experience of love and relationship. We are constantly called to die to our ego selves in order to experience life and love more fully. Woman's call for the feminization of world structures through the model of relationships of love and friendship must, therefore, include the dying process intrinsic to relationships of true love and friendship if that model is to be an authentic experience of new life possible for the human family.

Beyond Fear

Our fundamental vocation as Christians is to orient our entire being and life to God. The integration that we seek can come about only when we follow the intuition for otherness that places us in a relationship of love with the Divine Other and all others.

Decisions of the second moment of faith that lead us beyond egocentricity do not jettison us from one state to the point of arrival. Rather, the necessary turning from identification with the ego begins as we move toward otherness. It is a process and as such requires that we travel along the path that eventually leads to the place of arrival, namely, our being known and at one with Divine Being. It is this orientation toward God and the continued struggle to be faithful to it that give full meaning and purpose to life.

All who travel reflectively along this pathway notice periods of time when faith and its promises invigorate and motivate life, and times when a life of faith becomes dulled, as energies and enthusiasm for it diminish. At these latter periods in our life, we do not discount the reality of the presence of Divine Being, but we feel the absence of contact with God in our lives and conscious awareness. Frequently, out of the frustration we are experiencing, we challenge God to make God's presence known.

What we bring to our experience of the Divine Other is our

history of relationships and life. We therefore project onto God all the human fears and anxieties that are part of our experience. We are afraid, then, that perhaps this relationship, like our experiences in other relationships, will not be totally reliable; that our faith and trust are misplaced. We are afraid of being duped either by those practices of faith that promise to bring us into the realization of our relationship with the Divine Other, or by ourselves in believing that the reality of Divine Being is worth our total orientation and trust. Crassly put, "What's in it for me?" and, "Is it worth it?" can hallmark the path traveled by those pursuing a life of faith. We are afraid to let go and trust God completely because we fear that the people and things we need to make our life happy or bearable will not be provided. We fear that in letting go of self-preoccupation for Otherness we will know diminishment and deprivation. Frequently, those traveling along the way talk about "fear" as an amorphous condition that keeps them from total commitment, but they cannot, or will not, or do not, name exactly what they are afraid of.

Fear, however, is something to be reckoned with and not ignored because that is what imprisons the human heart and prevents it from experiencing known love. Therefore, fear must be acknowledged and dealt with before it can be transcended.

When the human heart turns toward the Divine Other in an act of mature faith, it embarks on a journey away from egocentricity into a reality beyond its own comprehension. It is a characteristic of human persons to be frightened by the unknown and by what they cannot control or imagine. Since the movement of the human heart toward Otherness seems different from what is known and clung to, it is a movement that produces fear. This fear, like so many of our fearful responses to life, stems from our trying to imagine the future and to project into it our present reality and anxieties.

However, because we are not catapulted from one state to the next by our "yes" to the invitation of Divine Love, the process itself happens within the context of our daily lives and the present moment. We, as it were, continually use our freedom to say "yes" in a context that allows a safe environment for confirming that Divine Love is trustworthy.

Those committed to this process frequently ask: "As you move toward the Divine Other, does your life become more virtuous? Are you freed from anger, greed, self-preoccupation, the compulsions of your life?" The answer to these questions is often disconcerting to those who raise them. In many of us there seems to be a subliminal desire to be perfect. But wanting to be perfect, even perfectly virtuous, can be another manifestation of egocentricity. Within the Christian tradition, there are mentors of faith who can shed light on the path we follow. From their lives and our own experience we learn that oneness with the Divine Other is already the present reality of all women and men. We know that our conscious awareness is blocked from that experience. Those seeming layers that separate us from becoming one with the reality of Divine Love in us are made up of the fears that cluster around certain aspects or issues of our lives. When these materials are allowed to surface into our conscious awareness, a movement from darkness and hiddenness into light, we can let go of them and no longer feel bound by them. These clusters of fear usually surround issues of sexuality, inferiority, authority, anger, identity, and death. Compulsions such as obsessive thinking alert us to the dominating experience of fear. Our fear is the result of identifying with a belief system concerning our identity. When we identify with egocentricity, our experience will be fear. When we identify with the true self, our experience will be love.

Since the orientation of ourselves toward the Divine Other is the process of discovering our true identity, it necessarily requires the undoing of a belief system that is the result of attaching ourselves to the perceptions and controls of egocentricity. Fear will be involved because it is precisely fear that caused us to repress and deny certain issues in our life.

· The dark night of the soul spoken about in classical works on spirituality can be the experience of a journeyer who in saying "yes" to the Divine Other simultaneously opens self to freedom from fear. The release from fear comes about when we open our conscious minds to the acknowledgment of what keeps us fearful.

St. John tells us that perfect love casts out fear. This means that when we are in the experience of true love, we will identify with a belief system that is true about ourselves and others. In it we will know the intimate and loving relationship we have in God. No clusters of fear exist in such a state because our fear is only possible when we use our freedom to separate ourselves from this truth.

We will indeed, because we are creatures and finite, experiment with experiencing ourselves as the center of the universe and not needing God. The gift of freedom allows us to do this, since the experience of true love is dependent on human freedom. Otherwise our seeming love is really servitude. We can, therefore, make choices other than orienting ourselves toward the Divine Other. The experience of these other choices becomes the hidden material of our conscious minds and consequently fills us with fear because we see in them the choice for egocentricity and a turning from Divine Love.

We consciously or unconsciously project onto God the experience of ourselves at such moments, which is the experience of self-loathing and perceived evil. We then believe this is God's experience of us as well. Because we cannot believe in our own lovableness, we do not believe in God's unsurpassable love for us. All of this contributes to the formation of clusters of fear and the forms in which fear is expressed.

And so, lurking in the hearts of those who make this decision of the second moment, which is a "yes" to Divine Otherness, are repressed fears. The pathway into Divine Love will eventually teach us that there is nothing to fear. But the in-between stages of that journey require us to bring to the surface the hidden material, and when we bring it to light, it will no longer be able to block our awareness of true love. And that is why on our spiritual journey it can often happen that our wholehearted response to Divine Love seems to make us more aware of our faults and self-preoccupation.

The material of our unconscious mind that locks us in fear will continue to surface until the false system of belief that we have identified with is undone. And so, rather than being a place of discouragement, the conscious awareness of the formerly hidden material of our life, although a source of difficulty or pain, can also be a source of great joy. It confirms the fact that we are indeed turned toward the Divine Other and that the layers that separate us from full participation in this Love are being penetrated.

The other dimension of fear that needs attention is the fact that fear produces fear. Those things that are hidden take on monumental proportions over time because of the energy that must be constantly used to repress them. Since the material was so heinous to us at the time we repressed it, we assume that allowing that same material to surface now will be overwhelming. We are afraid to deal with the material repressed when we were four, fourteen or twenty-eight years of age. We fear that what would have happened to us then if we did not repress this material will happen to us now.

Carol, age forty-two, a social worker, was watching a television program that depicted a family trying to function normally in spite of the mother's alcoholism. Carol identified immediately with the eight-year-old child in the film and for the first time admitted to herself that her mother was an alcoholic.

Susan, age thirty-eight, had spent most of her childhood not living up to her parents' expectations and remembers her mother always comparing her with others. Consequently, as an adult, Susan always felt inadequate and lived with the fear that people would experience her as superficial. Susan spent a great deal of energy compensating for this and warding off through defensive behavior what she felt as "life threatening." One day at a meeting, someone angrily accused Susan of being a superficial person. Susan recounts the story saying that her worst fear had happened and that to her surprise it wasn't devastating. In fact, she says, she felt freer after that than she had for years.

Each of the cases cited is an example of surfacing hidden material to consciousness and knowing new life because of it. Each of the people involved was able to handle, at this point in her developmental history, material that couldn't be handled in the past.

Entrusting oneself to the Divine Other will mean moments of, or periods of, dark nights—those times when our awareness seems flooded by our own fears and we feel captive within them, and times when the surfacing of the hidden material of our life can be so uncomfortable or painful because we begin to doubt, again, our true identity. At such times, we see played on the screens of our own conscious minds the unharnessed fears of our past. Now, however, we bring to this experience our history in faith, which has brought us to the point of our life where we have said "yes" to the Divine Other. We have learned that Divine Love is reliable and is trustworthy. We have experienced in myriad instances of our life the truth that love casts out fear.

The point at which our accumulated experiences and learnings about faith, life, and love converge is a place of enlightenment. It is the experience of the presence of Lady Wisdom (she who is the historically feminine portrayal of God) penetrating our perceptions and vision. It is she who now enables us to go beyond fear, toward Otherness.

In the Book of Wisdom, Solomon articulates for us the effects of Lady Wisdom:

❦ *Quick to anticipate those who desire her, she makes herself known to them. Watch for her early and you will have no trouble; you will find her sitting at your gates. Even to think about her is understanding fully grown; be on the alert for her and anxiety will quickly leave you (Wisdom 6:13–16).* ❦

Our decision to turn completely toward the Divine Other simultaneously releases not only our fears but also the gifts of God that we have repressed with them. Our "yes" allows God's hovering Spirit to freely intermingle with our identity. And so we meet the fears of our life not merely with our limited resources but in and with God's Spirit and gifts set loose in us.

Love, then, does not conquer fear, that is, control it or hold it in abeyance. Rather love undoes fear. It is the presence of the Spirit of Wisdom in our life that enables us to recognize this truth. It is she who leads us into the full realization of intimacy and union with Divine Love.

❦ *For within her is a spirit intelligent, holy, unique, manifold, subtle, active, incisive, unsullied, lucid, invulnerable, benevolent, sharp, irresistible, beneficent, loving to all, steadfast, dependable, unperturbed, almighty, all-surveying, penetrating all intelligent, pure and most subtle spirits; for Wisdom is quicker to move than any motion; she is so pure, she pervades and permeates all things.*

She is a breath of the power of God, pure emanation of the glory of the Almighty; hence nothing impure can find a way into her. She is a reflection of the eternal light, untarnished mirror of God's active power, image of God's goodness.

Although alone, she can do all; herself unchanging, she makes all things new. In each generation she passes into holy souls, she makes them friends of God and prophets; for God loves only those who live with Wisdom. She is indeed more splendid than the sun, she outshines all the constellations; compared with light, she takes first place, for light must yield to night, but over Wisdom evil can never triumph. She deploys her strength from one end of the earth to the other, ordering all things for good (Wisdom 7:22–30, 8:1). ❦

II

THE PRACTICE OF CHRISTIAN MEDITATION

Dark Night

Drunk
I am
with the
mellow wine
of sweet serenity
sipped in
misery
pain
rejection,
addicted
to the need
for mercy
that writhes
and cries
Son of David
pity, pity, pity

the terrored emptiness
resounds
echoes
its detonating sound
of
no sound

no sound
no touch

no look
no invitation
to my sycamore tree
        of pain—   of misery
Son of God,
pity, pity, pity

now
mellowed in wine
I am engulfed
swallowed
devoured
into being
other than mine,
The Divine—
the wine
of desert spent
night-souled place
(that luxury of excess)
of incomprehensibility
of all that is
and that is All—
pitied, pitied, pitied

Contemplative Prayer: The Essential Component of Mission and Ministry

God's reign in our world is dependent upon the conversion of the human heart. Without this necessary conversion, the structural changes brought about by "good works" eventually erode into evil systems that perpetuate different forms of injustice. Although conversion of the human heart and structural change must be worked for simultaneously, structural change remains the complement of the foundational change that burgeons systems of true peace and justice, namely, the conversion of the human heart. For our world to become a place where brothers and sisters are not deprived or ravaged economically, socially, and emotionally, the human heart must be turned from its propensity for egocentricity, which has produced the injustice and lack of peace experienced in our world.

Contemplation is the path to this necessary conversion of the human heart. The works of peace and justice become the activity of those who know the experience of authentic prayer.

WHY DO WE NEED CONTEMPLATION?

Contemplation is essential to the minister who proclaims the gospel and works for peace and justice in our world. Here are some reasons:

- Contemplation puts us in touch with our fundamental identity and the meaning of life—namely, that we are in intimate relationship with Divine Being and that our lives must be oriented toward the draw of Divine Love.

- Contemplation is essential to our nature as human persons. The depth of our humanness must be uncovered. At the root of human nature is wholeness and oneness in and with Divine Love. Without prayer that takes us beyond self-preoccupation, we are distracted from this truth and live with illusions about ourselves and the meaning of life.

- Through contemplation, we are re-membered to our primary relationship: our intimate bonding in Divine Love. Without contemplative prayer, we forget this and begin to act in this world without faith.

- The reign of God is contingent upon Christ's own ministry of healing, redeeming, and reconciling the human heart being carried out by present-day disciples. Since it must be Christ's ministry, not our own, it is necessary for us to do all that we can to become one with the mind of Christ.

- Ministers not continually renewed through the practice of contemplative prayer quickly burn out, lose faith, and become disheartened with the tasks and pain that are part of missionary life.

- Evil and suffering in the world continually confront a minister's faith. Seeing people suffer unnecessarily, and witnessing injustice and the many forms of oppression can create impasses of faith in a minister's life. The faithful practice of contemplative prayer breaks through the impasse to a place of vision and renewed energy for mission.

- If we do not incorporate contemplative prayer into the daily practice of life, we can easily lose contact with our essential nature (the true self) and begin to act and operate in our world as though we, not God working through us, could bring about the conversion of hearts and the necessary structural changes within world systems that complement this conversion. As we begin to rely more and more on our own efforts, ministry can suffer from the absence of faith: it can become faith-less.

• Ministers who do not acknowledge their contingency on Divine Being fail to have their own hearts converted—the essential element of the reign of God.

• If we do not steep ourselves in contemplative prayer, our ministry can become work into which we project our own egocentric needs and desires. We, as it were, become the center of the universe as our involvement and importance in the tasks of mission escalate. We begin to believe that the good that can be accomplished can only be done by us.

• Contemplative prayer is the acknowledgment of our ontological poverty. Through its practice, we become more conscious of our own utter dependence on God for all things, including life itself. Our dependence on the Divine Other awakens us to the common bond we share with all in the human family.

CONTEMPLATIVE PRAYER: CHRISTIAN MEDITATION

The path of contemplative prayer practiced through Christian meditation is the way of pure prayer because it involves the human person in the practice of self-forgetfulness that results in completely turning toward the Divine Other. Different forms of contemplative prayer encourage stilling our bodies and minds by initiating the prayer time with a quieting exercise, such as imagining ourselves going down an escalator and away from thought and imagination, or repeating a word or phrase until we feel silent.

Christian meditation urges the repetition of a mantra for the full meditation time of thirty minutes. The repetition of a mantra is an act of concentration that focuses our attention. It is a way of turning from our egos and is therefore a way of silencing all thought and imagination for the whole prayer period. The concentration we bring to the act of repeating our mantra acts like a searchlight that directs its beam away from the self to the word being said. Its practice enables a letting go of, or disconnecting from, egocentricity. In insisting that the mantra be repeated throughout the allotted prayer time, the tradition of Christian meditation provides a discipline that readies the heart for the complete turning toward the Divine Other, a turning free of egocenteredness. This practice of dying to the ego does not diminish or divest us of all the gifts and goodness that make us truly human; rather, this practice puts us in direct contact with the reality of our humanness—the true self.

Time is a human phenomenon. When we speak about contemplation, we are actually talking about a moment of prayer that prescinds all human boundaries, including time. The path of contemplative prayer readies us for the moment of true contemplation. This contemplative moment is an experience of God unmediated by images; it is an experience of knowing Otherness and becoming known to ourselves in that experience, and it is the experience of oneness in and with Divine Love. It is not an experience we control or cause. This union with the Divine Other is a reality already present to us that we realize when we are free from ego-centeredness.

Contemplative prayer, therefore, is the microcosm for the experience of life. We are all called to this practice because we were meant to live contemplative lives, lives that are Other-centered. By setting aside time each day for the practice of contemplative prayer, we act out what is foundational to our nature. It remembers us to the truth of our identity—the self found in an intimate relationship of love with Divine Being.

Authentic prayer as the experience of Divine Otherness will always lead us to others in ministry, love, and service. Love of God and love of neighbor are inseparable truths.

Authentic ministry is the result of contacting the reality of God's spirit present to us in our world and allowing that reality, rather than our own egos, to determine the shape and goals of ministerial activity.

Christian meditation is the opportunity for contemplative prayer that holds within it the way of aligning our consciousness with the consciousness of Christ through the practice of dying to our ego selves. It is a discipline that will eventually transform our entire lives as our realized oneness with Christ's own spirit becomes an ever present reality.

Hiding:
Dissatisfaction in
Prayer

Those traveling along the way can go through periods when prayer seems distasteful, unprofitable, or irrelevant. And so prayer as part of daily life is stopped or entered into halfheartedly. This lack of enthusiasm or conviction about prayer can have a variety of symptoms, but it usually has only one cause: guilt.

Guilt more than any other experience will influence our prayer life as well as our general sense of well-being. It is the experience of perceiving ourselves as an ego and not as our true self.

As such, we feel separated from what is the truth of our identity. Identifying with our egos is the result of a perception that indicts us as bad, evil, or unlovable, and fills us with self-hatred. This distorted perception of ourselves fills us with fear and anxiety. Not liking ourselves, we hide, afraid of being discovered. We hide from others, if not physically, then emotionally and psychologically, through our pretense and our masks, and we hide from God, as it were, by avoiding prayer. All this makes us feel more inauthentic and consequently more guilty. And the more guilty we feel, the more need we have not to be known, which produces the endless cycle of hiding, self-hatred, fear, and guilt.

This false perception of ourselves as ugly and evil keeps us ever more distant from the truth of our being, its lovableness and inherent goodness. The belief that we are not lovable holds us back from consciously presenting ourselves in prayer to Divine Love. Thus we project onto God the image we have of ourselves, with all our own limits. "God could not love me now," we say. It is a subtle form of idolatry—God made to fit our perceptions. Within such a perception, God's love cannot encompass us, nor can God's reconciling activity be our experience. This way of thinking, when reflected upon, is not that of a soul humbled in the experience of its creatureliness, as it might appear. Rather, it is an arrogant belief, one that determines the reality of God. Not praying, or suspending prayer until we can once again feel worthy, are both the ploys of an ego that keeps us turned in on ourselves and at the same time makes us feel distant from God.

We rarely perceive that we are identifying with our ego rather than our true selves as we travel along the way. Rather, we experience a symptom. We find in prayer an unprofitable experience. "I'm not getting anything out of it," "Nothing happens in my prayer," or "It's boring," are some ways of expressing this symptom.

Frequently on the spiritual journey, the moment of breakthrough—that is, the dismantling of a layer of the ego world that dulls our perception of the presence of Divine Reality—coincides with our moment of greatest pain and discouragement. The ego senses some form of death approaching as Divine Light penetrates the walls of egocentricity. The dis-ease of this experience is reflected in our pain.

It is important, therefore, to persevere in our commitment to Christian meditation and not to give way to discouragement on our journey. The pathway to Divine Light will, at times, seem dark and perhaps hopeless. Our very re-commitment to prayer at such times is the opening into light.

The Spiritual Journey

The essence of human nature is that it experiences its own finitude and limits as it is being drawn into the infinite and limitless experience of Divine Love. The spiritual journey is our conscious response to this attraction of Divine Life.

Our intuition tells us we have an identity that is truer than the identity we know or are experiencing. We become conscious of this reality usually around the age of thirty, when we experience dissatisfaction with and disbelief in those elements of our life that we initially thought would bring us completion or happiness. The disease we know causes us to look beyond the self that we are experiencing, which seems empty and devoid of meaning, and to bring our conscious minds now to the growing intuition inside ourselves that hints of the more to which we are called.

Psychological language would describe this as the tension between the ego or false self and the true self. The true self is that place where identity is realized. The ego or false self is that place where the attraction to the drawing of Divine Love is cut off and denied.

The ego becomes the source of its own life and identity. But because human nature is continually being drawn into the realization of a deeper and truer identity, cutting itself off from life results in the illusions of the ego. In seeing itself as the source of its own life, the ego lives a lie about its identity and purpose. The ego turns its energy to its own self and life sustenance. This turning away from Divine Life and living as though independent of that Life is in itself inauthentic. The ego or false self is the name ascribed to this phenomenon. It is important to note that schools of psychology use the term ego to describe the dynamics of human personality in other ways; as such, it is an arbitrary term, used to describe the mystery of human personality. The ego here will denote the false perception of a self as has been described.

Our spiritual journey is the life process. It is not something we do that is extrinsic to our life, nor is it made of moments in our life that focus us on God and spiritual concerns. Life is, of its nature, inherently spiritual because we are continually being called into Divine Life. The conscious attention we bring to this reality is our struggle not to define or experience ourselves as egos and to enter more deeply into experiencing the truth of our identity, which is the self known and found in God.

The Journey Toward Oneness: Stages of Christian Meditation

Our journey toward God and true identity involves a number of stages. These experiences are not essential to Christian meditation, but they are identified by some meditators as part of the process.

NOTICING

The realization that our egocentricity has not brought us, and cannot bring us, the fulfillment and completion that we are looking for awakens in our heart the consciousness of its own incompleteness. This experience of the need for something more expresses itself in the dissatisfaction we feel with the shallowness of our lives.

EXPLORING

Our desire for "something" that will give more meaning or purpose to our lives leads us to explore a variety of experiences that promise to give us the sense of well-being we are looking for. Our twentieth-century living provides us with supermarkets of experiences, canned and wrapped with assorted labels such as "Fitness Programs," "New Age Spirituality," or "Astrology." We choose one or several of these, looking for the "right fit." After we've spent time in one or many of the programs offered, the "shaping-up" of body, mind, or spirit that has occurred in them, however good for us and worthwhile, leaves us disappointed. The sense of incompleteness surfaces to our consciousness again.

CONTACTING

Our search for "that something" that will answer the spiritual hunger we are experiencing leads us to the teaching of Christian meditation, which will be explained in the chapters that follow. Perhaps it is through a colloquium on prayer, or a tape, or a book, or a friend that this teaching first comes to us, and with it, the intuition that this is what we are looking for. For some, a tension arises between this intuition and the fear of being duped. We address this tension by researching the authenticity and history of this prayer form in the Christian tradition.

CONNECTING

Our deep desire connects with a prayer form as a way of bringing us into the silence of an awakened heart, one that knows that it is in the presence of Total Being, Divine Love. We recognize the answer to our desire in the possibility open to us of self-realization in Divine Being. And so, filled with enthusiasm, we begin the daily practice of Christian meditation.

DISCOURAGEMENT

As we travel along the path of promise, we frequently encounter the discouragement of unrealized hope. Praying the mantra (the repetition of a word) continuously during our meditation periods is a discipline. We interpret as failure our lack of success at quieting our minds and imagination and obtaining stillness of body. We then begin to question whether this prayer form is meant for us, or whether it is so very different from the other products offered at the supermarkets of experience.

GIVING UP

Without the wisdom of a spiritual guide to help us on our journey, we may find that the ego can so dominate our perceptions of reality that we become controlled by our ego and its illusions. Because we feel we are not getting anything from the practice of prayer, we stop praying. The illusion of freedom can result from this decision because now we are freed from the work involved in this discipline, we are freed from the expectations we brought to the experience, we are freed from making the decision to pray each day. We are deceived by the ego into thinking that "being freed from" is equated with the experience of true freedom. The ego can keep us in this illusory state until we again realize that we are not freed from our desire for something more.

MORATORIUM

For a time we suspend our active search for truth and, consequently, for identity as we recover from failed expectations. This is not a denial of the draw of Divine Love nor a denial of the need to find oneness in Divine Intimacy. Rather, it is the suppression of both by one who no longer knows what to do. Until we know what path to follow, we place a moratorium on all that is spiritual.

RETURNING TO THE PAST

Our pilgrimage has a faith history. There were places along the way where we did sense God's presence and felt a sense of integrity free of the angst that is part of our present search. In an effort to recover what we once had, we return to the past. Wanting what was experienced then to be our experience now, we again identify with a particular religious practice or the site of a religious happening in our lives. We discover, however, that the experience or feeling we are seeking belonged to the past. We learn that only the present can express the incarnational moment of God's presence. The past experience is now only a memory. The experience no longer exists.

COMING OF AGE

The spiritual journey, like any other human endeavor, can be saturated by its own brand of self-preoccupation and selfishness. Seeking religious experience for its own sake is one of the manifestations of our ego-centeredness; demanding that God be known to us in the ways we have determined is another. The craftiness that is part of the ego's world can easily delude us into thinking that we can experience new life without entering into the death mystery that precedes it. Facing into the death mystery in faith not only prepares us for our final death and resurrected life, it also brings us into new life in the present. The coming of age on the spiritual journey has to do with a maturity of faith where we turn to and open ourselves to Divine Reality, trusting in the graciousness and love of that reality. It is the decision to let go of, to die to, our ego and its illusions and not project onto God what we think should happen in our prayer. Coming of age on the spiritual journey is indicated by our readiness to acknowledge and claim our own utter poverty and our total dependence on Divine Abundance for everything. It is a self-emptying experience (no matter how imperfect) that is willing to let go of seeking anything for itself, even experiences of God.

AWAKENING

Awakened to the fact that there is no separation, no distance between our full human identity and Divine Life, we return to the practice of Christian meditation and to our original intuition of its rightness as a way of realizing this truth. We now recognize Christian meditation as a discipline whose practice is congruent with our desire to die to our egos. Each period of prayer becomes the symbolic acting out of this decision and the acknowledgment of our utter poverty. We no longer approach prayer questioning what is in it for us, since (to the extent that this is possible) we now go to it free of desire for, and expectation of, anything. Our complete surrender to Divine Abundance is an act of total dependence on God. Our awakened heart now sees the prayer periods as times within the day when our complete attention is given over to the drawing of Divine Love to which we consciously respond.

COMMITMENT TO THE PRACTICE OF MEDITATION

Our commitment to the practice of meditation comes not only from the recognition of this prayer form as grounded in the truth expressed within the rich and long history of Christian tradition but also from the validation of our own experience in it. We discover in it a path that leads to the uncovering of all that keeps us from being fully human. Through this process of self-forgetfulness, which is the dying of the ego, we enter a place of silence in which our true identity is realized. Essentially, this religious practice, like all religious practice, is concerned with relationship. The faithful practice of meditation brings us to the awareness of our being in the being of God.

EXULTATION

Penetrating the layers of egocentricity not only brings us into the discovery of our own identity but simultaneously brings us into a place, although still veiled from our complete awareness, of knowing. Knowing, as such, is not an experience of something, but is Reality realized. Out of this muted realization, joy and exultation become part of our being and flow into and energize our life. As our conscious awareness is expanded into Reality, our commitment to the process of meditation is strengthened. This is because the knowing that is realized simultaneously makes us aware of what is yet unknown.

The Phases of Christian Meditation

The first phase of Christian meditation brings us into relationship with Christ. God's spirit expressed in Jesus is present in all human life. Therefore, we know that the same spirit present in Jesus is present in us. To be drawn into Divine Presence is to be in contact, however veiled, with this spirit of Jesus. Like the people in the gospel who approached Jesus in faith, through our contact with Divine Life we are brought into loving relationship with Christ, whose ministry continues its healing, redeeming, and reconciling activity in us.

In other words, as our relationship with Christ deepens, we are freed from the shackles of our ego perceptions, which distort our image of ourselves and our images of the world family. Relationship with Jesus (like all true love relationships) and the heightened experiences of love we know in and through Jesus help us to begin to experience ourselves as God does—loved completely and without limits. When this is the experience of an individual, the good news of the gospel becomes the lived experience of that person. Our ministry in the world is the direct result of our encounter with Jesus and the transformative power of this realized love.

The second phase of Christian meditation is the experience

of becoming one with the consciousness of Christ. We are joined to Christ's own prayer already being prayed in us, which is the unveiling of God's reign in the incarnational moment of the present.

The practice of Christian meditation does not make the relationship with the Divine Other happen. It has already happened. Rather, what we do through the practice of our prayer is to come into an awareness of our being in Divine Being. We awaken to the presence of Divine Love. The draw of Divine Love brings us ever deeper into this Reality.

As the self comprehends its true identity, it realizes that Divine Love is trustworthy and so entrusts its very self to it. The draw of Divine Love, unblocked by obstacles, is the place where the self is known and at one with God. Christ is the example of this experience. The prayer of Christ, that is, Christ's own consciousness, becomes the experience open to every woman and man.

The great fear among modern day women and men is that their individuality will be submerged or lost. Their personal histories make them suspicious of anything that would crush human potential or deny human experience. It is only by in-depth human discernment that we are able to distinguish the voice that comes from our identification with the world of our egos from the voice of Truth and Reality.

The path of Christian meditation is a way into the experience of oneness. Our relationship with Christ brings us to the realization of our true identity. The experience of our true identity is the experience of oneness with the consciousness of Christ.

The Expansion of Consciousness: The Experience of the Meditator

We act on intuition for Otherness and the turning from egocentricity each time we enter into the practice of Christian meditation. When we are faithful to the practice of meditation, Christ's own consciousness becomes our experience. We see ourselves and our world through new eyes, the eyes of faith.

Through the use of a mantra (a repeated word), we focus our attention. Our total concentration on the mantra leads us beyond egocentricity to a place of utter stillness, a place of self-forgetfulness. The quieting of our bodies, minds, and imaginations leads us to a reality beyond our own known experience.

The time spent in meditation is itself an act of faith. Nothing is supposed to happen during our prayer periods (thirty minutes each morning and evening is suggested) except that we continue to concentrate by saying our mantra. We are informed by the tradition of Christian meditation that no experience, not even what seems like religious experience, should be given our attention during this prayer time. The teachers of the practice of Christian meditation tell us to simply and gently return to repeating our mantra for the full half hour of our meditation.

Those steeped in the rich treasures of Christian spirituality know that any experience of God is an experience of a divided consciousness. The ultimate nature of human life is that it is one with God, which is an experience of undivided consciousness. It is the experience of the self, not reflecting on God, but knowing itself in God.

Christian tradition uncovers and presents this prayer practice as a way open to those who seek oneness with the Divine Other, but the practice itself must be experienced as authentic by those engaging in it as they journey on the path toward Oneness.

And although nothing happens during the practice of Christian meditation, because it is an act of self-forgetfulness going beyond ego preoccupation, there are ways of registering that the path we have chosen is an authentic one and is leading us more deeply into Divine Otherness. These indicators confirm a new realization of the presence of God's Spirit intermingling with our identity and affirm our intuition that the way of Christian meditation leads us into truth.

Those who are new to the practice of Christian meditation will find it necessary, then, after they have spent a significant period of time in the faithful practice of Christian meditation, practicing it each morning and evening, to assess their own experience of commitment to this practice. Although this assessment still hints of self-preoccupation, it is necessary. We must find in the tradition and in our own experience the assurance that eventually leads us to self-forgetfulness and other-centeredness.

The indicators of God's Spirit that manifest themselves outside of our prayer time in our daily lives are increased faith, deeper love, and greater hope. The particular ways these gifts are manifested will vary with individuals.

The manifestations of God's Spirit in our experience are the result of an awakened consciousness.

PERCEPTION

Seeing differently or with the eyes of faith indicates a shift in our conscious awareness that enables us to be different. As our minds and hearts gradually become one with the mind and heart of Christ, everything seems to change. Because we are moving toward our true identity, a place where we are found in the love of the Divine Other, the reality of love that is now our experience gets extended. Consequently, as we begin to experience oneness, we feel more connected to others. Sisterhood and brotherhood become realized truths.

POVERTY

Our meditation alerts us to both God's unsurpassable love and our own self-preoccupation and egocentricity. As we become more aware of the invitation of the Divine Draw, we also become aware of our choices to live as though we, not God, are the center of life, as though our life's meaning is the immediate and constant gratification of our own egos. We realize that, left to our own resources, we would continually use our freedom inappropriately and in ways that produce misery and its own forms of death. Recognizing our own limits and finitude, we know poverty. We know how poor we are and how dependent we are on Divine Love to redeem us from the self-created bondage of our ego selves. We know also that the completion that we desperately long for can be found only in God, and that we are helpless in saving ourselves. All that we can do is offer our willingness, our "yes" to Divine Love.

PEACE

There is nothing more sought after and desired in our time than the gift of peace—interior peace and world peace. Interior peace is the gift of a heart that knows the experience of Divine Love. When we are no longer afraid, no longer caught in the guilt and anxiety that block our experience of love, we know peace. Peace is the result of handing over our very lives to the Divine Other, knowing that Divine Love is completely trustworthy and that all we need will be provided—that there is nothing to fear. Because it is indigenous to human nature to extend what is known in its own heart, the experience of interior peace that we now know is extended in our world. We become peacemakers.

FORGIVENESS

Because we have experienced our own poverty and our redemption in it, we develop hearts continually involved in the process of forgiveness. Recalling our own egocentricity, and our remembrance of the misery and fear we have known as part of it, helps us to be merciful and forgiving toward others. We know that our own misperceived experience of being cut off from Divine Love because of our egocentric pursuits resulted in behavior that projected our fear and self-hatred onto others. Our forgiveness of others is the extension of our own known experience of mercy. It is the extension of love to others who seem out of touch with their true selves. We have the ability to extend love and join with others, even those who on one level seem undeserving of our love and attention, because we are sharing in Christ's own consciousness. Like Christ, we do not ignore or repress our awareness of the manifestations of others' egocentric behaviors displayed in attack, domination, control, misuse of power, or preservation of their own lives over and against the lives of others. But, like Christ, we begin to recognize this behavior as the result of feeling separated from one's true self. We know from our own experience that it is only the power of love that redeems us and draws us beyond our egocentric pursuits. We, therefore, understand that we participate in redemption, are co-redeemers, as we extend the love that has healed, redeemed, and reconciled us. We, by our love, participate in awakening the consciousness of others to their true identity.

OTHERNESS AND OTHERS

Our relationship with the Divine Other will always move us to relationships with others in a life of love and service. Since our prayer leads us into Christ's own consciousness, our life will pattern what was most characteristic of Jesus' life, a life of relationship and service to the Other and all others. Like Jesus, our life will grow in its expression of the inseparableness of love of God and love of neighbor as we allow ourselves to be drawn more deeply into intimate relationship with the Divine Other.

The path of Christian meditation leads us to a place of silence in which we are joined with the Spirit of Jesus already praying in us. Each time we enter the practice of Christian meditation, we release ourselves in loving faith to the Divine Other, entrusting ourselves to Divine Abundance in an act that is self-emptying. This response of self-forgetful love (not to be confused with self-rejection) corresponds to the desire of Divine Love to have us participate in the fullness of its own life.

Those who have chosen the path of Christian meditation as the way to intimate union with the Divine Other will know from their own experience that their faithful commitment to the practice of this prayer has brought them to a more conscious awareness of the life of the Divine Other and their relationship in love with others.

How to Meditate

Dear Companion Along the Way,

The method of Christian meditation is utterly simple. Here are some guidelines for its practice:

• Choose a place where you know you can be sure of the most silence possible.

• Sit still and upright.

• Close your eyes lightly.

• Sit relaxed but alert.

• Silently, interiorly, begin to say a single word. The recommended prayer phrase is *Maranatha*. Say it as four equally stressed syllables: MA RA NA THA.

• Concentrate on saying the word continuously.

• Do not think or imagine anything, spiritual or otherwise.

• If thoughts or images come, these are distractions at the time of meditation, so gently return to the exercise of concentration by repeating the mantra.

• Meditate morning and evening for between twenty and thirty minutes. Decide on the time before beginning, and complete the allotted time period.

Don't be discouraged because you seem to maintain your concentration on the mantra only for minimal periods of time.

Each time you pray, remember that meditation is an act of self-forgetfulness. Do not, then, allow your prayer to become another instance of egocentricity by registering it under the titles of success and failure after you have completed it. Rather, enter into it each time with simplicity of heart, giving yourself to the experience as completely as you can and without anxiety. It is a prayer of faith. Trust, then, in Divine Love and God's hovering Spirit leading you to the promised land of truth and identity found in Divine Otherness.

With affection,
Eileen

III

REFLECTIONS FOR THE JOURNEY

Mantra Prayer

penetrating love
cuts
dissolves
surrounds
abounds
    is one.
uncovered
discovered
the vagabond
is found
in sound

ejected
coaxed
driven
    beyond
hearing
fearing
seeing
being
clamorous stillness
unfleshes
    the word
birthing
oneness.
unknowing.

The Purpose
of the
Reflections

Dear Companion Along the Way,

Each of the following reflections on Scripture is meant to be read immediately before the daily prayer periods. It is my hope that the content within each will resonate with your own experience and thereby encourage you in faith in the practice of Christian meditation.

These reflections are meant to move the heart into the practice of prayer where the desire for oneness in Divine Being becomes more than a good idea. We stop talking about, reading about, and thinking about prayer. We do it. We act on our intuition, and through the practice of Christian meditation and the repetition of our mantra—Maranatha—enter the silence where Divine Otherness is realized.

Listening to the taped conferences of John Main over ten years ago affirmed an intuition within me that oneness with the Divine Other was possible and essential. It is my hope that these reflections will encourage the journeyer to persevere in the practice of Christian meditation and to see it as a way to full consciousness. Because Christian meditation is a pathway to identity realized in relationship to Divine Love, it uncovers the full potential of all that is good and true within us. The feminine and masculine in each of us is realized in this process.

The quieting of mind, imagination, and body that is required for Christian meditation in no way diminishes our human potential. Rather, because it brings us beyond our false self or ego, we consequently know greater being and our consciousness becomes expanded.

Christian meditation presents "the way" to those who realize their desire for total commitment has been on the periphery of their lives for too long and that it is time to say "yes" and entrust oneself completely to Divine Love. Each time we meditate we say this "yes."

Because Christian meditation is a discipline, it takes commitment and perseverance. It is my hope that these reflections will spark the energy of desire already in your heart.

With affection,
Eileen

Phoebe, Prisca, and Aquila: Women in Ministry

❧ I commend to you our sister Phoebe, a deaconess of the church at Cenchreae. Give her, in union with the Lord, a welcome worthy of saints, and help her with anything she needs: she has looked after a great many people, myself included.

My greetings to Prisca and Aquila, my fellow workers in Christ Jesus who risked death to save my life: I am not the only one to owe them a debt of gratitude, all the churches among the pagans do as well. My greetings also to the church that meets at their house (Romans 16:1–5). ❧

Women's intuition for otherness is well represented in the women Phoebe, Prisca, and Aquila. In them we find a commitment to the gospel evidenced in their generosity and other-centeredness. These women are remembered by name because their significant role in the formation of the Church at Rome was noteworthy.

Woman's intuition for otherness then and now leads her to seek after truth and to participate in unveiling God's reign. In our modern world, the predominance of women in our churches—at centers for spiritual direction, at courses for psychological and spiritual development—confirms the insight of women's heightened capacity for otherness.

Women and those men whose experience incorporates a female system of belief desire and pursue ways of being in intimate relationship with the Divine Other. In Phoebe, a deaconess in the Church, and Prisca and Aquila, we find lives of service. They opened their hearts and homes, even risking death, for the sake of the Gospel.

In our own time, women's concern that the good news of the gospel be proclaimed has resulted in their active participation in the work of justice and peace. Christian commitment for twentieth-century women means selfless service, particularly to the socially and religiously abandoned. It means uncovering all the roots of injustice that keep us from realizing our oneness as a human family.

All systems of oppression—sexual, social, and economic—will be addressed by women because oppressive systems are the antithesis of a model of universal love and friendship as preached and lived by Christ. Women know that to be in intimate relationship with the Divine Other necessarily involves a life of loving relationship and service to others. Therefore, women actively participate in freeing themselves and others from the oppression of patriarchal systems because of the misuse of power and the inequality of persons perpetuated through them. Women know that the true identity of both women and men is denied by such systems as well as by those who find it necessary to perpetuate them.

Phoebe, Prisca, and Aquila are among the few women remembered by name in the Gospel text and acknowledged for their contribution to the formation of the Church. Perhaps they, like modern-day women, had to step out of the roles assigned them by patriarchal and cultural systems in order to follow their intuition in the pursuit of truth and dedicated service.

All who are dedicated to the works of justice and peace in our world know that their dedicated service to others can be both life-giving and death-dealing. It is life-giving at those moments when we sense our own utter poverty and because of it experience a oneness with God and others in a ministry that is mutual. It can be death-dealing when despair and discouragement seem to take over as our own efforts do not produce the desired good.

The prayer of Christian meditation keeps our vision clear and energizes us with the faith, hope, and love necessary for our journey. The self-emptying experience of Christian meditation, in which we turn completely toward the Divine Other, leads us to the encounter with God's Spirit in us. It is this experience of knowing oneness with the Spirit of Jesus, that enables us to work confidently for the unveiling of God's reign despite the hardships. In and with this Spirit, we, like Phoebe, Prisca, and Aquila, participate in and continue Christ's own ministry.

Let us now, through the self-emptying experience of Christian meditation, which is the realization of our own utter poverty, turn our hearts and minds completely toward the Divine Other.

Intimacy:
The Human Family

His mother and brothers now arrived and, standing outside, sent in a messenger asking for him. A crowd was sitting round him at the time the message was passed to him. "Your mother and brothers and sisters are outside asking for you." He replied, "Who are my mother and my brothers?" And looking round at those sitting in a circle about him, he said, "here are my mother and my brothers. Anyone who does the will of God, that person is my brother and sister and mother" (Mark 3:31–35).

Belonging is a basic human need. We want to know that there are significant others in our lives on whom we can depend. We want to know that there are people who love us and will continue to love us, no matter what happens. The fear of abandonment is deeply rooted in the human psyche and can taunt all our relationships with the threat of loss. Commitments to love made in relationships are the ways we human beings try to address our need to be loved by someone forever. The experience of committed love diminishes but never totally destroys the threat of loss we fear. The realization of our own finitude and limits is part of all human endeavors and as such casts its shadow over our relationships. Egoism can so abuse and distort love that the very commitments we thought were final dissolve or end abruptly. We long for the safety of secure relationships where love is experienced as never ending.

In Mark's gospel account of Jesus, we find the theme of relationship directly addressed. The need to be in relationship with and loved by others is as apparent in the life of Jesus as it is in ours. The importance of his mother Mary throughout Jesus' life is attested to by her identified presence in all the accounts of the gospel writers. The importance for Jesus of belonging and love are underscored by the key relationships in his life, which portray various levels of intimacy and love. Jesus' frequent visits to Bethany and his relationships with Martha, Mary, and Lazarus are examples. Jesus' unique relationship with some of his disciples—namely, Mary Magdalene, Peter, James, and John—is another.

When Jesus in this gospel account looks at those sitting in a circle about him and says, "Here are my mother and my brothers [and sisters]," he is not shunning those he so deeply loves; rather, he uses the very experience of intimate relationships as the paradigm for revealing the truth that this setting occasioned.

By incorporating those in the circle into a place formerly reserved for family, he expands the human and fragile experience of loving by identifying it as intimately connected with the Divine. The love that we humans feel we need is not in juxtaposition with Divine Love, nor separate from it. Loving relationships and the experience of true intimacy in our life carries us more deeply into the reality of Love, which is the place where the essence of human and Divine life are one.

Christian meditation is the practice individuals commit themselves to in an effort to enter the experience of true love, free of the distorted images and concepts of the ego. The gentle repetition of our mantra is a way of stilling our minds and imaginations of false ego perceptions and entering into a place of deep silence where truth exists free of distortion. The continued practice of meditation is the path that leads us to a love so encompassing that the aspects of threat and loss construed by our egos as essential to love become identified as illusions. As a result, our need to love and be loved by others is more fully realized as we experience our oneness with Divine Reality.

Let us now through our meditation and the gentle repetition of our mantra enter onto the path that leads to the experience of complete intimacy as we more fully realize the oneness that is our identity.

Joanna:
Generosity of Heart

&❧ *Now after this he made his way through towns and villages preaching, and proclaiming the Good News of the kingdom of God. With him went the Twelve, as well as certain women who had been cured of evil spirits and ailments; Mary surnamed the Magdalene, from whom seven demons had gone out, Joanna the wife of Herod's steward Chuza, Susanna, and several others who provided for them out of their own resources (Luke 8:1–3).* ❧*

Joanna is mentioned by name in this account and again in the resurrection narrative. We know that she was one of Christ's disciples and that she used her money to help support him and his followers. Joanna reminds us that Jesus was free to preach the Good News because he was enabled to do so by generous people like herself.

An encounter with a generous heart is always refreshing. We recognize in it a God-like quality because Divine Abundance is continually expressing itself to humankind in limitless love. Jesus is the manifest outpouring of this love.

The instinct for Divine Life that was in Joanna recognized Jesus as the way to God. And so, she gave of herself and she gave of her means. Her generosity is the result of an awakened heart. Although there is no doubt that Jesus must have had a profound effect on Joanna that resulted in her discipleship and support, she is, nevertheless, remembered because of what she did for Jesus.

Joanna, then, is a paradigm for us of a generous heart. She is not remembered for her words to Christ or about Christ. She is remembered because she participated in his ministry through her discipleship, which enabled him to proclaim God's reign.

When we pray our Christian meditation, the instinct we have for Divine Life is acted upon. Through the repetition of our mantra, we try to empty ourselves of selfish preoccupation so that we may be opened to Divine Abundance. It is our openness to unsurpassable love that releases in us a generosity of heart that is so much part of our true identity. Through the path of Christian meditation, we are drawn into Christ's own prayer that is being prayed in us. Our discipleship and ministry witness to this continued presence of Christ in our world.

Let us then put our love into action by entering into our prayer. Through the gentle repetition of our mantra, let us quiet our bodies and our minds of all the stimuli bombarding us and open ourselves to the experience of Divine Abundance, found in the stillness of our heart.

The Woman Who
Stands Straight:
The Reign of Love

ঌ . . . *she was bent double and quite unable to stand upright. When Jesus saw her he called her over and said, "Woman, you are rid of your infirmity" and he laid his hands on her. And at once she straightened up, and she glorified God (Luke 13:10–13).* ঌ

Scripture as God's word spoken into human history communicates God's message revealed in Jesus and to his followers. Because it is a living word, its power incorporates and transcends the historical moment in which it was spoken. In this gospel, Jesus affirms that the compassion of God transcends boundaries made by people, and that a lack of health and wholeness is not part of God's design. Jesus restores the woman to health by ridding her of her infirmity, her bent back.

A parallel is frequently made between this woman and women bent low by oppressive structures throughout the centuries. Like the synagogue officials of Jesus' time, there are many who focus their attention not on God's action working through her and the miracle of Divine Love made visible in her wholeness, but on the manmade regulations of religious or cultural practice.

When true love for others is not the operating principle of relationship between women and men, it is replaced by fear, which manifests itself in competition, domination, and control. True love, as represented in Jesus, is always concerned for the good of the other and has no need to use the other or things outside itself, such as the law, to validate itself and its worth.

Jesus' adversaries were threatened because he did not keep the law that dictated to them how they were to live in this world. In keeping the law, they felt affirmed and righteous. If the law could be transcended, it meant that their righteousness within the law could be questioned.

Modern-day woman is standing tall in her reclaimed identity. This identity, too, has become threatening to those who felt safer finding her bent low by social and cultural conditioning that regulated her gifts and identity. Finding some sense of security or comfort in another's infirmities is not an infrequent response to life, although its manifestations are often more subtle and obscure. The heart that is fear-filled is uncomfortable around wellness and wholeness because it is there that it confronts its own lacks. We make comparisons that result in feelings of superiority, for example, we are more well than . . . more psychologically sound than . . . from a healthier family than . . . richer than . . . All are attempts to balance out the threat of inferiority lurking in our hearts.

The message of Jesus for all times is that love must reign in the human heart. When love becomes the core from which our actions flow, neither diminishing others nor feeling diminished by them is necessary. Neither competition nor submission is required. The heart that is rooted in love stands tall, secure in its own identity. It rejoices that others are standing tall too.

It is this joining of our identities in the wholeness of truth that this Gospel text re-members us to. It is love given and received that heals the woman of her infirmity, and it is love given and received that will heal us of our infirmity—fear.

The path of Christian meditation leads us beyond our fear to a place of realized love. It is a way that leads us to knowing the oneness that we share with all women and men.

So let us now, through the gentle repetition of our mantra, silence our minds and imaginations and enter that sacred space of knowing.

Tabitha:
Discipleship

❧ *At Jaffa there was a woman disciple called Tabitha, or Dorcas in Greek, who never tired of doing good or giving in charity. But the time came when she got ill and died, and they washed her and laid her out in a room upstairs. . . . on [Peter's] arrival they took him to the upstairs room, where all the widows stood round him in tears, showing him tunics and other clothes Dorcas had made when she was with them. Peter sent them all out of the room and knelt down and prayed. Then he turned to the dead woman and said, "Tabitha, stand up." She opened her eyes, looked at Peter and sat up. Peter helped her to her feet. Then he called in the saints and widows and showed them she was alive. The whole of Jaffa heard about it and many believed in the Lord.*

Peter stayed on some time in Jaffa, lodging with a leather-tanner called Simon (Acts 9:36–43). ❧

The story of the woman disciple Tabitha portrays the intimate connection between faith and the death mystery. What Jesus did for humanity, unshackling us from the bonds of death, is evidenced in the power that enabled Tabitha to be called forth from death.

As Christians, we consciously participate not only in faith *in* Jesus but also in the faith *of* Jesus. It was the faith of Jesus that allowed him to freely accept death and enter into it, thereby breaking the bonds in which death held the human heart. It was death and the fear of death that kept humanity unfree, trapped in egoism.

The universal deliverance of God mediated through the crucified and risen Jesus unshackled humanity from death's bondage. That death has lost its power over humanity is shown when Tabitha is raised from the dead at Jaffa, among its new Christian community.

Only in the risen Jesus do we glimpse what it is like to experience the new life that goes beyond death, a life that calls us beyond finitude. The promise of new life after death transcends limited human experience, which remains bound in its ego until death has been accepted and entered into.

Tabitha points the way to the hope of new life because in her we see a power operating that is greater than death. Since it is the fear of death that keeps us shackled, Tabitha exemplifies the truth that the new life we long for is opened to us and that the death that kept us from it can be passed through.

There are very few women disciples named by the writers of Scripture. Tabitha is one of them. Her discipleship continues today because what is preached through her is the link between faith, death, and Christian commitment. In Tabitha, a faith lesson for human history is made explicit.

The life of faith and love that Tabitha lived as a disciple is a catalyst for this happening. Tabitha is described as a woman who never tired of doing good, one deeply loved by others, one who shared her talents in ministry; her friends showed Peter the tunics and other clothes Tabitha had made.

Unlike Tabitha, we modern-day disciples frequently grow tired of doing good, and faith becomes not the vital motivation of life but a muted belief or a dulled conviction. Our spirit and ministry often reflect the diminishment of faith.

Since faith and the mystery of death are so intimately connected, we can easily discover that the diminishment of faith, or the lack of motivation for the journey we are experiencing, is directly connected to patterns of death denial and destructive death avoidance going on in our life. This includes the deaths that are part of our dying every day and our final death.

Tabitha portrays in her discipleship an other-centeredness that indicates a dying to egocentricity. If we wish to be highly motivated and enthusiastic in our discipleship, then we, like Tabitha, must be willing to live into the death mystery by dying to our ego-centeredness. This is possible because Jesus, in breaking the bonds of death, opened a pathway that leads beyond egocentricity. Through Jesus, we are enabled to turn toward the Divine Other. In so doing, we are energized by Divine Life and experience a joy and peace that come from the penetration of a Reality greater than our own egos.

When we enter into the prayer of Christian meditation, we turn toward the Divine Other. Each time we meditate, we consciously enter into a death experience as we die to egocentricity and self-preoccupation and allow Divine Life to draw us beyond the ego-self we usually experience.

Every meditation period, of its nature, is a self-emptying experience. It is an experience where finitude and limits are acknowledged and dependence on Infinite Being realized. The continued practice of meditation leads us beyond our own egos to a place of self-realization where the new life promised becomes known, although still veiled, as we begin to experience the faith of Jesus present in us.

Let us pray now, with the hope and love that knows Divine Being is trustworthy and enter our meditation ready to open ourselves completely to Divine Life.

Martha:
Bonding

ᴥ *There was a man named Lazarus who lived in the village of Bethany with the two sisters, Mary and Martha, and he was ill. . . . The sisters sent this message to Jesus, "Lord, the man you love is ill." On receiving the message, Jesus said, "This sickness will end not in death but in God's glory, and through it the Son of God will be glorified."*

Jesus loved Martha and her sister and Lazarus, yet when he heard that Lazarus was ill he stayed where he was for two more days before saying to the disciples, "Let us go to Judaea." The disciples said, "Rabbi, it is not long since the Jews wanted to stone you; are you going back again?" Jesus replied: "Are there not twelve hours in the day? A man can walk in the daytime without stumbling because he has the light of this world to see by; but if he walks at night he stumbles, because there is no light to guide him."

He said that and then added, "Our friend Lazarus is resting, I am going to wake him." The disciples said to him, "Lord, if he is able to rest he is sure to get better." The phrase Jesus used referred to the death of Lazarus, but they thought that by "rest" he meant "sleep," so Jesus put it plainly, "Lazarus is dead; and for your sake I am glad I was not there because now you will believe. But let us go to him." Then Thomas—known as the Twin—said to the other disciples, "Let us go too, and die with him."

On arriving, Jesus found that Lazarus had been in the tomb for four days already.... When Martha heard that Jesus had come she went to meet him. Mary remained sitting in the house. Martha said to Jesus, "If you had been here, my brother would not have died, but I know that, even now, whatever you ask of God, he will grant you." "Your brother" said Jesus to her "will rise again." Martha said, "I know he will rise again at the resurrection on the last day." Jesus said: "I am the resurrection. If anyone believes in me, even though he dies he will live, and whoever lives and believes in me will never die. Do you believe this?"

"Yes, Lord," she said "I believe that you are the Christ, the Son of God, the one who was to come into this world."

When she had said this, she went and called her sister Mary, saying in a low voice, "The Master is here and wants to see you." Hearing this, Mary got up quickly and went to him....

Mary went to Jesus, and as soon as she saw him she threw herself at his feet, saying, "Lord, if you had been here, my brother would not have died." At the sight of her tears, and those of the Jews who followed her, Jesus said in great distress, with a sigh that came straight from the heart, "Where have you put him?" They said, "Lord, come and see." Jesus wept; and the Jews said, "See how much he loved him!" But there were some who remarked, "He opened the eyes of the blind man, could he not have prevented this man's death?" Still sighing, Jesus reached the tomb: it was a cave with a stone to close the opening. Jesus said, "Take the stone away." Martha said to him, "Lord, by now he will smell; this is the fourth day." Jesus replied, "Have I not told you that if you believe you will see the glory of God?" So they took away the stone. Then Jesus lifted up his eyes and said: "Father, I thank you for hearing my prayer. I knew indeed that you always hear me, but I speak for the sake of all these who stand round me, so that they may believe it was you who sent me."

When he had said this, he cried in a loud voice, "Lazarus, here! Come out!" The dead man came out, his feet and hands bound with bands of stuff and a cloth round his face. Jesus said to them, "Unbind him, let him go free" (John 11:1–44). ❧

Relationships of true love and friendship are seen in the bonding that existed among Jesus, Martha, Mary, and Lazarus. In them we recognize the experience of love, an experience that goes beyond words to a sense of truly knowing the other.

Jesus has compassion for Martha and Mary both because he loves them and because of the depth of his own sorrow. He experienced the feeling of loss because of the absence of one he loved.

Martha and Mary's love for Jesus seems to incorporate the

total person of Jesus. He was their close friend, and the depth of this love for Jesus brought them to a realization of the presence of God in him.

In our relationships with others, our perceptions of them frequently are quite limited. We therefore categorize them or confine them to lifetime scripts that keep them bound. Often, much of our relating is not part of the process of true love but is a using of the other for the sole purpose of filling our own neediness and egocentric pursuits. Our vision of them is limited to what they can be or do for us. In such cases, we don't truly love others but use them to distract ourselves from the experience of our emptiness and guilt.

A model of true love and friendship is represented in Jesus, Martha, and Mary. Their love is other-centered, not self-centered. In Martha we see a love for Jesus that evidences a depth of knowledge and understanding of him. Martha said to Jesus: "If you had been here, my brother would not have died, but I know, even now, whatever you ask of God, he will grant you."

We sense that both Martha and Mary had come to know Jesus well. That is why they realized the power of God in Jesus. "Yes, Lord," Martha said, "I believe you are the Christ, the Son of God, the one who was to come into this world." And Martha knew that what was beyond human imagining could happen through Jesus. She knew that the impossible could happen—that her brother could be raised from the dead.

We discover that Martha's deep relationship with Jesus brought her into an experience in which her consciousness was expanded. Her awareness that Jesus could call her brother forth from death transcended limited human knowledge and experience.

Martha represents for us, therefore, one of the effects of relationship with Jesus. All who enter into an intimate relationship of love with Jesus are changed by that experience. For Martha the expansion of consciousness she knew because of this relationship meant that she was no longer confined to some limited perceptions; that is, she now knew a power greater than death; the seemingly impossible was now possible.

Frequently, we are confronted by happenings in life that seem impossible to work out. They can be issues of relationship, ministry, or world concerns. We can, because of them, feel trapped, overwhelmed, and hopeless.

In Martha we find a woman whose perceptions were no longer limited solely by human conditioning. Because of her loving relationship with Jesus and others, she had an expanded vision of reality and could see with the eyes of faith.

Christian meditation is a way of becoming one with the consciousness of Christ that enables a shift in consciousness to occur. Through it we begin to see with the eyes of faith, no longer limited by perceptions and belief systems that are solely the result of our human conditioning. Through the continued repetition of our mantra, we enter a place of silence where we join the prayer of Jesus being prayed in us. From this vantage point of faith we experience reality differently—the impossible becomes possible in faith.

Let us now enter our prayer with the faith that takes us beyond human imagining and limits.

The Woman and Man Who Committed Adultery: Stands for Justice and Peace

They all went home, and Jesus went to the Mount of Olives. At daybreak he appeared in the Temple again; and as all the people came to him, he sat down and began to teach them.

The scribes and Pharisees brought a woman along who had been caught committing adultery; and making her stand there in full view of everybody, they said to Jesus, "Master, this woman was caught in the very act of committing adultery, and Moses has ordered us in the Law to condemn women like this to death by stoning. What have you to say?" They asked him this as a test, looking for something to use against him. . . . As they persisted with their question, he looked up and said, "If there is one among you who has not sinned, let him be the first to throw a stone at her." Then he bent down and wrote on the ground again. When they heard this they went away one by one, beginning with the eldest, until Jesus was left alone with the woman, who remained standing there. He looked up and said, "Woman, where are they? Has no one condemned you?" "No one, sir" she replied. "Neither do I condemn you," said Jesus "go away, and don't sin any more" (John 8:1–11).

In this scripture reading, Jesus is tested by the scribes and Pharisees, who are looking for something to use against him. When we are told that they present to him a woman caught in the act of adultery, we sense that the woman has been spoken of and used as an object. Little attention or significance is paid to her as a person or to the feelings she must have been experiencing through this public humiliation.

The man involved in this act of adultery is not mentioned because he was not judged as sinful by the law. Sexual and cultural discrimination account for the fact that the same act is judged differently for women and men.

The scribes and Pharisees had a great investment in seeing this woman as evil and in having Jesus condemn her. In them we recognize something that can easily happen in ourselves. Frequently, we too want to prove or demonstrate that someone is evil and should be condemned. And we want others to see that person as we do. So gripped are we by our own egocentricity that our hurt, anger or hate seem to have a life of their own. Proving the other wrong, unlovable, or evil, we believe, will vindicate our suffering and pain. It sometimes happens that we have invested so much of our ego-self in fostering a certain perception of the other that we seem unable to disconnect from it even when it is recognized as untrue or damaging and unhealthy for us. We become victims of our perceptions.

This is what seems to have happened to these scribes and Pharisees. They use the woman as a way to destroy their perceived enemy, Jesus. They would have affirmed that the law of Moses, as they interpreted it, transcended the model of love and relationship that Jesus lived and preached. If Jesus did not abide by the law and condemn this woman, they had the needed evidence to condemn him.

Jesus, however, refuses to condemn the woman. He does not see her as evil and worthy of stoning. Rather, he challenges the scribes and Pharisees' perceptions of her by inviting those who have no sin to be the first to attack the sin in this woman.

In Jesus, we discover a response to personal attack that is nonviolent, and we discover someone able to confront the existing oppressive structures without hatred toward the perpetrators. Jesus takes strong stands for truth, stands that will eventually result in an ignominious death.

We are taught through Jesus' whole life that we too must take stands for truth. These stands might make us marginal people in the eyes of the world, cause discomfort, or even result in death for the sake of the gospel. Jesus' adherence to principles of love and friendship as the model for life never prevented him from confronting the evils of his time but, in fact, motivated that response.

For us, learning how to take strong stands on issues of justice and peace while remaining in the experience of love is difficult. Loving our enemies and those who oppress and hurt us is more difficult.

The oneness Jesus experienced with Divine Love made this possible for him as it will for us. It is the experience of oneness with God, and consequently with all women and men (otherwise it is not oneness), that accounts for a response of love even to those who are reacting to life out of egocentricity.

The ideal of nonviolence and a universal model of love and friendship are things we value and admire. Jesus teaches us that this value will be a reality in our lives to the extent that we are in communion with the Divine Other and others.

Through the practice of Christian meditation every morning and evening, we direct our full consciousness to this reality. Through our prayer, we consciously attend to letting go of our egocentric thoughts and images of ourselves and others and turn completely toward Divine Love as the source of our life. The practice of Christian meditation is, therefore, the way that re-members us to the truth of our identity, which is the self known and found in love. It is this experience of ourselves that then allows us to see others in the truth of their being. We recognize that they, too, are known and found in love even though their behavior indicates that they have chosen to disassociate themselves from the conscious awareness of this truth.

It is vital, then, for us if we are to know true peace and love, both interiorly and in our world, that we persevere in our commitment to prayer as the way of re-membering us to truth. Our stands for justice and peace will be motivated then by the experience of oneness with the Divine Other and all others.

Let us now through the practice of Christian meditation turn completely toward the Divine Other, where we are indeed re-membered in truth and love.

The Woman Who Was Hemorrhaging: Transcending Shame

❧ *Now there was a woman suffering from a hemorrhage for twelve years, whom no one had been able to cure. She came up behind him and touched the fringe of his cloak; and the hemorrhage stopped at that instant. Jesus said, "Who touched me?" When they all denied that they had, Peter and his companions said, "Master, it is the crowds round you, pushing." But Jesus said, "Somebody touched me. I felt that power had gone out from me." Seeing herself discovered, the woman came forward trembling, and falling at his feet explained in front of all the people why she had touched him and how she had been cured at that very moment. "My daughter," he said, "your faith has restored you to health; go in peace" (Luke 8:43–48).* ❧

Filled with shame over her hemorrhaging, which was considered a legal impurity (Leviticus 15:25), the woman of this gospel reaches out and touches Jesus. Her intuition, which recognized in Jesus a source of cure, transcended the boundaries of culture and legal tradition as she made contact with him. The law was strict regarding a man with a seminal discharge or a woman with a discharge of blood. Both were seen as unclean: the person with the discharge and those who touched him or her. The woman's shame comes not only because of her biological condition, but also because now, according to Jewish law, Jesus has been made unclean by her touch.

Jesus searches for her in the crowd because her intuition has been only partially realized in the cure that has been effected. Jesus is not content that a healing has taken place, since his ministry is not about good works alone but the faith that brings about the deeper healing.

Frequently, cultural and/or family conditioning confine us to images of ourselves, as it did for this woman in the gospel. These images fill us with shame and self-loathing. The ego uses these feelings to keep us from realizing a deeper and truer dimension of self, which is in contact with the sacred.

As we travel along "the way" and find ourselves caught in some compulsion, our guilt and self-hatred keep us locked in the experience of shame that perpetuates and increases the cycle of guilt and self-hatred.

This woman of the gospel has much to teach us. Her instinct for wholeness forced her beyond predetermined boundaries. This acting on her intuition brought her into healing and relationship with Christ: "My daughter," he said, "your faith has restored you to health . . ."

If we extricate ourselves from God's light when we are stuck in our compulsions, if we wait until we feel we are clean enough to encounter Christ, or if we wait to expose ourselves to the light only when our ego tells us we are in the proper condition to do so, we will miss the healing that is extended to us. We must be open for it to be effected in us.

When we pray our mantra in Christian meditation, that healing becomes a reality in our life. Through the means of this self-emptying prayer, we come in contact with Divine Love, which heals every wound and brings us beyond our woundedness to a true self discovered in love.

Coming to oneness with our true identity is the experience of wholeness and health where compulsivity and shame no longer exist.

So let us now place ourselves in that healing light as we enter into the silence of our meditation, using our mantra as the way of entering into the silence and leaving the preoccupation with false ego behind.

Mary of Magdala: New Life

❧ *Meanwhile Mary stayed outside near the tomb, weeping. Then, still weeping, she stooped to look inside, and saw two angels in white sitting where the body of Jesus had been, one at the head, the other at the feet. They said, "Woman, why are you weeping?" "They have taken my Lord away" she replied "and I don't know where they have put him." As she said this she turned round and saw Jesus standing there, though she did not recognize him. Jesus said, "Woman, why are you weeping? Who are you looking for?" Supposing him to be the gardener, she said, "Sir, if you have taken him away, tell me where you have put him, and I will go and remove him." Jesus said, "Mary!" She knew him then and said to him in Hebrew, "Rabbuni!"—which means Master. Jesus said to her, "Do not cling to me, because I have not yet ascended to the Father. But go and find the brothers, and tell them: I am ascending to my Father and your Father, to my God and your God." So Mary of Magdala went and told the disciples that she had seen the Lord and that he had said these things to her (John 20:11–18).* ❧

Mary of Magdala does not recognize Jesus in this scripture account until her name is spoken. Her response then is a spontaneous act of love—she reaches out to hold the beloved. Mary's exuberance and desperation are manifested by her desire to cling to Jesus. In this act, it seems that the overwhelming sense of loss Mary was undergoing was instantly alleviated by Jesus' returned presence in her life. When Jesus instructs her, "Do not cling to me, because I have not yet ascended . . ." he confronts Mary with the change that has occurred. He identifies in himself a new experience for human life, a new way of being—life that goes beyond death. Jesus, as savior, has broken the chains of death that shackle humankind's hearts and envelop them in fear so great that they repress thoughts of death and deny its reality as an integral part of human life.

Jesus' salvific teaching, first to Mary and then to the other apostles and disciples, is that it is precisely through death that new life comes. Sin occurs when humankind refuses and denies death as an integral part of life. Since we human beings are finite, we experience in varying degrees the infinite expansion to which we are continually called but which we can fully realize only when we have entered into the death mystery.

In reporting to the others what she had seen and heard, Mary proclaims the Good News that, in Jesus, humanity is now freed from the shackles of death. We can safely surmise that something must have changed in Mary as well that set her free of clinging and enabled her to be the first to witness to and proclaim that Jesus had risen from the dead.

Another paradigm for the death mystery and new life can be found in the interaction between Jesus and Mary. What Mary knew concerning the felt experience of love and relationship had been circumscribed by the culture of human patterning. But what Mary was to learn, and we through her, is that even what is deepest and truest in us—our intuitions about love and loving relationships—is still influenced by the perceptions of an ego constantly involved in its own immortality project. Mary's attempt to cling to Jesus can be seen as her refusal to admit that anything had changed. For her, it would seem, fear and a sense of loss and deprivation were synonymous with change. And so she clung, not wanting to lose what she knew and loved.

Because the Mary we meet at the end of this account is no longer clinging but going to spread the Good News to others, we know change has occurred. Mary must have trusted the love that Jesus had for her enough to allow her heart to be open to the newness of their relationship. Mature love does that and knows that it must be open to change if it is to deepen and expand.

In not clinging to Jesus, Mary had to let go of—that is, die to—her ego perceptions of what she thought she needed and wanted from the relationship. She clung because she so desired what she once had. However, Christ's love for Mary drew her into an experience of love and relationship that she could not have imagined or previously known. She now becomes the authentic witness to and proclaimer of the Risen One, because she too has experienced in their encounter the new life that Christ is announcing.

There are many deathlike experiences in each of our lives that prepare us for final death and the hope that we can bring to that experience. Each time we meditate, we enter some form of the death mystery. The continued repetition of the mantra is a way of silencing the distorted perceptions of the ego that distract us from an intimate encounter with Divine Love. Dying to our ego perceptions leads us into our true identity, whose source of life and energy is rooted in Divine Love itself. And because, like Mary, we have experienced the new life that comes from this encounter, we will stop clinging to egocentricity and go out to others and witness to and proclaim what we have experienced, the Risen One.

As we begin our meditation, let us trust Divine Love enough and open our hearts to this love by silencing our ego with the gentle repetition of our own mantra—*Maranatha*.

Mary of Nazareth:
Religious Experience

My soul proclaims your greatness, O my God,
and my spirit has rejoiced in you, my Savior,

For your regard has blessed me,
poor, and a serving woman.

From this day all generations
will call me blessed,

For you, who are mighty, have made me great.
Most Holy be your Name.

Your mercy is on those who fear you
throughout all generations.

You have showed strength with your arm.
You have scattered the proud in their hearts' fantasy.

You have put down the mighty from their seat,
and have lifted up the powerless.

You have filled the hungry with good things,
and have sent the rich away empty.

You, remembering your mercy,
have helped your people Israel—

As you promised Abraham and Sarah.
Mercy to their children, forever

(Companion to the Breviary,
Teresa M. Boersig, O.C.D.).

When we hear Mary's song of praise, which echoes Isaiah's longing (Isaiah 61:10), we know that these words well up from some deep experience of wonder and delight. Mary represents all humanity's desires and longing that find fulfillment in the experience of God in Jesus.

When the drawing into Divine Love is not blocked by our egos, we know moments of delight, ecstasy, and joy that are replicated in Mary's Magnificat because we, too, are experiencing God's presence in our lives.

The process of life that is our spiritual journey is the saving act of Jesus, penetrating human existence. It is creature being called to Creator, it is limited and finite human life being drawn into limitless love and infinite life. The experience of these moments along the way, those moments when we glimpse something beyond ourselves, those moments when we know there is a path leading us out of darkness into light, are moments of unsurpassable joy and hope. The Incarnation of Jesus, and all that means to human life, becomes part of our own lived experience at such times. These moments of realization give us the faith and hope necessary to carry us more deeply into the mystery of human life until we come to the next new moment of realization.

Mary teaches us something about the disposition of an individual in relationship to God when she says: "Be it done unto me according to your word." She teaches us to be open to God and God's revelation in our life according to God's designs, not ours.

Although God's revelation in and through us will find form in all that is our human conditioning, the experience of God surpasses all human experience. As such, any experience of God is not God—it remains our experience of God. The deepest and truest God experience is best represented in knowing. The truth of our being is that we are in communion, are one with God in the now, the present moment, of our lives. This is knowing. It is the everlasting moment, the timeless moment of Incarnation, realized, known, in our lives.

When we enter into our prayer of Christian meditation, we put aside the greed of our egos that would have us pursue experience, even religious experience, for its own sake. When we try to free ourselves of the illusions of our ego that could confine us to a world made to our own image and likeness, we, like Mary, open ourselves to the penetration of Divine Love. The gentle repetition of our mantra for two half-hour periods daily is a way of acknowledging and entering into experience that goes beyond our own limited perceptions. Christian meditation is a way of first encountering the Spirit of Jesus in us and in our world, and then entering into Christ's own experience, which is the experience of knowing.

Let us now, through our practice of Christian meditation, open ourselves to the eternal moment of God's love.

Mary at Bethany:
Loving

&❧ *Six days before the Passover, Jesus went to Bethany where Lazarus was, whom he had raised from the dead. They gave a dinner for him there; Martha waited on them and Lazarus was among those at table. Mary brought in a pound of very costly ointment, pure nard, and with it anointed the feet of Jesus, wiping them with her hair; the house was full of the scent of the ointment (John 12:1–4).* ❧

At the center of our being is the Reality of pure Love. The more awakened we become to this reality, the more it finds expression in our relationships and ministry. Mary's anointing of Jesus at Bethany is an example of love in action and intuition given form.

True love yearns to express itself.

As we penetrate more deeply the Reality of Love in us, we yearn for more complete contact. As we grow in our awareness of God's unsurpassable love for us and experience it in the depths of our being, we need and desire to respond with the fullness of our being.

It is indigenous to love that the experience be communicated. Mary's relationship with Christ brought her into the reality of profound love. Her response to that experience was, figuratively and literally, an outpouring of love seeking form and expression.

Mary's anointing is neither tolerated nor endured by Jesus. Rather it is received by Jesus as it is—love responding to love. Jesus not only defends this action of Mary but also acknowledges it as part of the gospel that he wishes preached. Mary's response to love is the gospel message received.

"I tell you solemnly, wherever throughout all the world the Good News is proclaimed, what she has done will be told also, in remembrance of her" (Mark 14:9).

As our relationship with Christ deepens and consequently our understanding of the reality of Love grows, it, too, will demand outpouring. That outpouring will be the compassion and love we "are" in ministry and relationship. To enter more deeply into that reality means awakening into the very life and prayer of Christ. This is precisely where Christian meditation leads us.

Our meditation time is our response to the experience of love. Repeating the mantra frees our minds and hearts of all other experiences and brings us to the point of undistractedness, where Love is more fully realized.

And so, let us enter into love with an awakened heart as we begin our meditation.

Jesus:
Intuition

🐾 *The Word was made flesh, he lived among us, and we saw his glory, the glory that is his as the only Son of the Father, full of grace and truth (John 1:14).* 🐾

We can think of Jesus as God's intuition given form, clothing that reality in human flesh and becoming just like us. The key to Jesus' ministry was relationship. What exactly did Jesus do? Why were there some people not cured, freed of demons, or left unbelieving when they had the opportunity to meet Jesus?

When we talk about intuition in ourselves, we mean those moments of real knowing that come not so much from reason or knowledge but from something that seems to bypass rational thought, registering deep inside us as true.

We all have experienced that in some way. It is the experience of being in touch with a broader vision of life and faith, and knowing its rightness—its truth.

Jesus in his ministry seemed to have that effect on his followers. Encountering him put them in touch with something that, deep within them, resonated as true. But why didn't Jesus have this effect on all whom he encountered? Probably because they were not open to the relationship, and as a result the intuition within them was blocked. Therefore, the necessary engagement with Jesus that would trigger this registering of truth, an intuition, was thwarted.

Like the match, the stove, and the gas jet, all that is needed for a flame to burst out and become a reality is present. Once the match is lit, however, nothing will happen until the valve is opened and the meeting of gas stream and lighted match takes place. At that meeting, something—a flame and steady stream of heat—comes into existence.

Each time we enter meditation, we place ourselves in a more conscious way in that posture that signifies our total openness to our relationship with God and our availability to the spirit of Jesus that is the center of our being. Through the practice of Christian meditation, our intuition becomes unblocked, and we begin to experience ourselves and all reality from a center of truth that is the shared life of Christ.

Let us enter our prayer now, fully open to relationship with the Divine Other, and through the repetition of our mantra join the silence deep within us where we are one with God's own Spirit.

The Woman from Canaan: Expansion of Consciousness

❧ *Jesus left that place and withdrew to the region of Tyre and Sidon. Then out came a Canaanite woman from that district and started shouting, "Sir, Son of David, take pity on me! My daughter is tormented by a devil." But he answered her not a word. And his disciples went and pleaded with him. "Give her what she wants," they said "because she is shouting after us." He said in reply, "I was sent only to the lost sheep of the House of Israel." But the woman had come up and was kneeling at his feet. "Lord," she said "help me." He replied, "It is not fair to take the children's food and throw it to the house-dogs." She retorted, "Ah yes, sir; but even house-dogs can eat the scraps that fall from their master's table." Then Jesus answered, "Woman, you have great faith. Let your wish be granted." And from that moment her daughter was well again (Matthew 15:21– 28).* ❧

One of the eventual fruits of our perseverance in Christian meditation is an expansion of consciousness. We all seem to intuit that there is something more to life than we are experiencing— another level of being or living that we sense but don't seem to be in contact with. The restlessness that we experience and try to quench in some activity is the soul's longing for something that comes in contact with a depth of being not yet experienced. Jesus' encounter with the woman from Canaan not only brought about a cure for the woman's daughter but also broke through a cultural barrier that, until he met this woman, circumscribed his ministry. Until this point, Jesus had perceived this ministry as confined to the Jews, not open to pagans. His contact with this woman, hearing her question, challenges him to place a traditional category of belief in the context of greater truth, namely relationship with a God whom Jesus experienced as Abba.

In Jesus' humanity we see the possibility open to all humanity. In him we see the effect of union with the Reality challenge the experience and categories that have been established through culture and tradition. In this account, we glimpse what the evangelization of culture looks like as the consciousness and identity of Jesus is more fully awakened to his relationship with his Abba.

That restless longing to be in contact with the More in our life is the call of the Spirit of Jesus in us to that oneness with this same Reality.

The practice of Christian meditation each day is the discipline that evangelizes our categories and perceptions by bringing us into contact with the Source of all Reality.

Three elements of listening seem present in the gospel scene: Jesus hears the woman's plea; Jesus hears his disciples intercede for her; and Jesus hears the voice of Love spoken within him.

As we pray our mantra, repeating it from the time we begin our meditation until its end, we approach a point of perfect stillness that allows us to hear the voice of Love spoken in us and in our relationships and causes the expansion of consciousness we long for.

As we enter our prayer, let us be attentive to hearing the voice of love in us through the gentle repetition of our mantra: *Maranatha.*

The Spirit of God: Experiencing the Void

As we travel along the way into the depth of light, we frequently experience darkness, dryness, or even depression. It is here that we can easily sink into despair and give up the pursuit because, for us, it has become like a formless void, immersed in darkness.

The opening lines of scripture address this very condition.

❧ *In the beginning, God created the heavens and the earth. Now the earth was a formless void, there was a darkness over the deep, and God's spirit hovered over the water (Genesis 1:1–2).* ❧

Scripture here and in several other places teaches us something that is peculiar to the working of the Spirit. That is, it is in just such places that God's Spirit hovers. The word "hovers" implies much more than a passive presence. Rather, we sense a charged presence ready to act.

Christian meditation is the act of the individual—whether that person is experiencing darkness or light—deliberately and consciously placing self in this hovering presence. Repeating the mantra becomes a way of penetrating the darkness and coming to that place of utter stillness and quiet that connects us to the charged presence of the Spirit, generating a life and vitality that exceeds anything imaginable.

Dryness in prayer, acedia as it is called in tradition, or the lack of feeling or insight experienced during prayer, are not major concerns to those who pursue the path of Christian meditation. In meditation, we leave all thought processes and all imagination behind us and choose instead to enter the depth of utter silence, where the spark of our being and the Spirit combust into wisdom, light, and life. It is not uncommon that the pull toward egocentricity dupes us into despair and discouragement the nearer we are to this happening. The ego is invested in its own life and knows that continuation in prayer brings us beyond egoism to a life in God.

The very place of discouragement for us is often the sign that we are coming close to more intense life. That is why most spiritual breakthroughs are preceded by intense discomfort. Someone once said that the thing we fear more than death is resurrection, or self-transcendence. And that is also why we must, in faith, plod through the experience with continued faithfulness to the Christian practice of meditation.

And so, let us enter this prayer time in faith.

The Prophets
Anna and Simeon:
Vision

ર [Anna] was now eighty-four years old and never left the Temple, serving God night and day with fasting and prayer. She came by just at that moment and began to praise God; and she spoke of the child to all who looked forward to the deliverance of Jerusalem (Luke 2:37–38).

[Simeon] was an upright and devout man; he looked forward to Israel's comforting and the Holy Spirit on him. It had been revealed to him by the Holy Spirit that he would not see death until he had set eyes on the Christ of the Lord. Prompted by the Spirit he came to the Temple; and when the parents brought in the child Jesus to do for him what the Law required, he took him into his arms and blessed God and he said: "Now, Master, you can let your servant go in peace, just as you promised; Because my eyes have seen the salvation which you have prepared for all the nations to see, a light to enlighten the pagans and the glory of your people Israel" (Luke 2:25–32). ર

When Mary and Joseph, in fulfillment of the Law, present the child Jesus in the Temple, both Anna and Simeon identify him as the expected Messiah and the fulfillment of the plan of salvation. As prophets, they recognize and reveal a truth of God to others. Both Anna and Simeon are described in sacred scripture as devout and prayerful people. With them, as with the prophets of the Hebrew scriptures, we see the interconnection between the words they speak and their own lives.

The gift of prophecy present in Anna and Simeon enabled them to see differently. They saw in a baby God's plan of salvation being fulfilled.

To live our Christian commitment in this world, we, too, must see differently. If we see only what our eyes experience, we will sink into disillusionment, depression, or despair. To see with the vision of faith means to see the redeeming act of Jesus at work, reconciling human hearts and bringing to completion the salvation promised and foretold by Anna and Simeon.

When we are left to our own resources, our inability to see with the vision of faith becomes evident in the places of unforgiveness in our lives as well as in the hopelessness we experience when viewing the world we live in. To see differently, with the eyes of faith, never implies distorting reality. It does not mean pretending the world we live in is not filled with pain and suffering, when that is our experience.

It is precisely these experiences, however, that bring us to the realization that, when we are left to our own resources, this is the only vision we are capable of. Bluntly stated, we are stuck, entrenched in the perceptions of our egos. The prophecies of Anna and Simeon reveal that we are not left to our own resources. Rather, what they prophesied would happen in Jesus is now the reality we share—it is now our inheritance. Through Christ, the bonds that shackled the human spirit have been broken. We no longer have to be enslaved by our perceptions and sinfulness. There is a way out. Because of Jesus, the possibility of seeing differently, of perceiving the truth of God, knowing God, is now open to us. If we have fastened onto a misperception—about ourselves, another, or our world—we can be drawn out of it because a power greater than humanity's sinfulness has penetrated the human condition.

The necessary disposition for seeing differently is faith, a faith in which the self willingly turns its freedom toward Divine Love and opens itself to its healing and penetrating power. It is this conversion of the human heart that brings about the process of our seeing differently.

In the practice of Christian meditation, our human heart freely turns toward Divine Reality. The silence that we are eventually brought to by this continued practice is not a soundless vacuum. It is rather a silence that transcends ordinary human perception, because in it, through the quieting of our minds of self-preoccupation, we realize Divine Otherness.

In this experience of being present to and known by Divine Being, the truth of our self (our true self) is actualized. The "seeing differently" that occurs is no longer something we try to do but is reality perceived by us from a new place of being.

Let us now, in our meditation, turn our heart fully to the Divine Other and through the continued repetition of our mantra begin the journey into silence.

The Women at the Tomb: Remembering

   On the first day of the week, at the first sign of dawn, they went to the tomb with the spices they had prepared. They found that the stone had been rolled away from the tomb, but on entering discovered that the body of the Lord Jesus was not there. As they stood there not knowing what to think, two men in brilliant clothes suddenly appeared at their side. Terrified, the women lowered their eyes. But the two men said to them, "Why look among the dead for someone who is alive? He is not here; he has risen. Remember what he told you when he was still in Galilee: that the Son of Man had to be handed over into the power of sinful men and be crucified, and rise again on the third day." And they remembered his words (Luke 24:1–8).

As we travel along the way, our life experience is often similar to that of the women at the tomb. Like them, we often know confusion and disappointment because what we had expected is not our experience.

These women, because of their love and devotion to Jesus, came to the tomb with the spices necessary to complete the ritual of embalming. Their relationship of love with Jesus did not terminate with his physical death. Their loving incorporated the reality of death.

The reality of death continually intersects our lives as well—

the death of those we love or the tomblike experience of failed expectations. Death in all its forms challenges our faith more than any other experience.

Long ago, most of us have stopped imagining the spiritual journey as so many steppingstones of growth leading to perfection. A more realistic image seems to be that of concentric circles that converge at a point deep within. Each circle represents the layers of ourselves that must be passed through until the full realization of our being converges and knows itself in Divine Being. And it seems that the penetration of each new layer is preceded by moments of utter darkness and bewilderment. We feel caught in fear and anxiety, tormented by the darkness of egocentricity. Often, we project our anger onto God, feeling that God has not cared well enough for us, has not protected us from the darkness we are experiencing, or has abandoned us.

The rich history of Christian spirituality can be a great comfort to us at such times, as well as the companionship of a spiritual guide. Both will remind us of the necessary death experience that precedes the experience of new life. Both will assure us that the terror we are experiencing is not God's design but our emotional response to what we are perceiving as life threatening. Because we have for so long identified with our egos, any movement away from egocentricity and our known experience fills us with fear and even a sense of dread.

Those gifted companions in faith, those who know the presence of Lady Wisdom, will remind us at such times, as the women at the tomb were reminded, to remember Christ's words. This is the lesson the women at the tomb can teach us as we travel along on our spiritual journey. After their experience of being shocked and terrified because their expectations were unmet, they were able to adjust to a new reality by one simple act: "They remembered his words." When they were re-membered to a truth deep within themselves, everything fell into place. Now freed of their own preconceived perceptions and expectations, they could enter a new layer of consciousness. They could now enjoy the peace and joy of a new reality—Jesus, risen from the dead.

When we are re-membered to the Word of God spoken in us, we, too, experience a freedom from fear and anxiety, and we know the joy and peace of life in God. Our "yes" in faith to Divine Otherness when death impinges on our life, re-members us to the truth of our identity. Death, then, is passed through, our consciousness expands, and we know the joy and peace of a new reality. We are now closer to the center of ourselves, which means we are more aware of our oneness in Divine Life.

Christian meditation is a direct way of re-membering ourselves to God's word spoken in us. By the faithful repetition of our mantra for the full time of our meditation, we eventually come to a place of stillness where we are joined with the Spirit praying in us.

Let us now begin our prayer by re-membering ourselves to God's word spoken in us: *Maranatha*.

The Woman from Samaria: Dialogue

❧ *When Jesus heard that the Pharisees had found out that he was making and baptizing more disciples than John—though in fact it was his disciples who baptized, not Jesus himself—he left Judaea and went back to Galilee. This meant that he had to cross Samaria.*

On the way he came to the Samaritan town called Sychar, near the land that Jacob gave to his son Joseph. Jacob's well is there and Jesus, tired by the journey, sat straight down by the well. It was about the sixth hour. When a Samaritan woman came to draw water, Jesus said to her, "Give me a drink." His disciples had gone into the town to buy food. The Samaritan woman said to him, "What? You are a Jew and you ask me, a Samaritan, for a drink?"—Jews, in fact, do not associate with Samaritans. Jesus replied: "If you only knew what God is offering and who it is that is saying to you: Give me a drink, you would have been the one to ask, and he would have given you living water."

"You have no bucket, sir," she answered "and the well is deep: how could you get this living water? Are you a greater man than our father Jacob who gave us this well and drank from it himself with his sons and his cattle?" Jesus replied: "Whoever drinks this water will get thirsty again; but anyone who drinks the water that I shall give will never be thirsty again: the water that I shall give will turn into a spring inside him, welling up to eternal life."

"Sir," said the woman "give me some of that water, so that I may never get thirsty and never have to come here again to draw water." "Go and call your husband" said Jesus to her "and come back here." The woman answered, "I have no husband." He said to her, "You are right to say, 'I have no husband'; for although you have had five, the one you have now is not your husband. You spoke the truth there." "I see you are a prophet, sir" said the woman. "Our fathers worshipped on this mountain, while you say that Jerusalem is the place where one ought to worship." Jesus said: "Believe me, woman, the hour is coming when you will worship the Father neither on this mountain nor in Jerusalem. You worship what you do not know; we worship what we do know; for salvation comes from the Jews. But the hour will come—in fact it is here already—when true worshippers will worship the Father in spirit and truth: that is the kind of worshipper the Father wants. God is spirit, and those who worship must worship in spirit and truth."

The woman said to him, "I know that Messiah—that is, Christ—is coming; and when he comes he will tell us everything." "I who am speaking to you," said Jesus "I am he."

At this point his disciples returned, and were surprised to find him speaking to a woman, though none of them asked, "What do you want from her?" or, "Why are you talking to her?" The woman put down her water jar and hurried back to the town to tell the people, "Come and see a man who has told me everything I ever did; I wonder if he is the Christ?" This brought people out of the town and they started walking towards him. . . .

Many Samaritans of that town had believed in him on the strength of the woman's testimony when she said, "He told me all I have ever done," so, when the Samaritans came up to him, they begged him to stay with them. He stayed for two days, and when he spoke to them many more came to believe; and they said to the woman, "Now we no longer believe because of what you told us; we have heard him ourselves and we know that he really is the saviour of the world" (John 4:1–30, 39–42).

The differences that we note in another or in groups of people very often keep us separated from one another and therefore not in relationships of love and friendship. In the dialogue that occurs between Jesus and the woman from Samaria, we find differences acknowledged and transcended. The woman of Samaria confronts an existing prejudice when she says, "What? You are a Jew and you ask me, a Samaritan, for a drink?" As their dialogue continues, we find it an expression of faith in which cultural differences do not inhibit an exchange in truth, which, of its nature can never be limited to or the sole possession of any group. Rather, the oneness in truth that is the ultimate nature of women and men is expressed in this conversation between Jesus and the woman of Samaria.

Because of others, we are not left in the experience of our own isolation, but through them we are drawn into a deeper knowledge and truth, where we experience knowing and being known in relationship.

Entering into truthful dialogue with another means a willingness to be open to the other. Frequently, we build so many defenses against the other because of our differences that truthful dialogue is hampered by our own fear and mistrust.

The woman of Samaria models for us what can happen when we are willing to approach one another undefensively, without fear that the thoughts or beliefs of the other will have the power to diminish us or our beliefs. The intuition of this woman from Samaria enables her to recognize in Jesus someone who is trustworthy. Jesus, in turn, in initiating this conversation transcends religious bias, which taught that Samaritans were to be hated because their religious practices still incorporated some loyalty to pagan gods.

In both Jesus and the woman, therefore, we find a history of religious and emotional patterning that accentuated the belief that differences created boundaries and prevented relationships.

Their dialogue underscores for us the fact that when truth is shared through dialogue, greater understanding and knowledge come about. For Jesus, and for human history, this dialogue brought about the articulation that Jesus is the Christ, the Messiah. For the woman from Samaria this encounter led her to a deeper reality of faith: "I wonder if he is the Christ?" Her community is affected by her experience as well: "Now we no longer believe because of what you have told us; we have heard him ourselves and we know that he really is the saviour of the world."

The story of the woman from Samaria highlights again woman's intuition for otherness that is translated into her desire and ability to enter into dialogue and share her experiences with another. Communication is the way of becoming known to another and therefore is an essential element of relationship. God's desire to express self and to be in a relationship of love and friendship with women and men is expressed in the very person of Jesus. In

Jesus, God's self is communicated. We, therefore, address Jesus as the Word of God.

For our dialogue with another to be an authentic exchange leading to a deeper reality, we must communicate a sense of ourselves, free of masks and pretense—our true selves. Another element necessary for true dialogue is our ability to allow the other's communication to enter our awareness, free of interferences from us.

The woman from Samaria models for us the listening and the self-communication essential to relationships of love and friendship that bring us to a deeper experience of reality.

The practice of Christian meditation is a way of joining in relationship with the Divine Other at a level of faith and love that takes us beyond words. Each period of our prayer of Christian meditation is a time when we entrust ourselves completely to the Divine Other, and through the quieting of our minds and imaginations enter into the silence where God's self-communication can be realized, free of interference from us.

Let us then enter in faith this time of prayer by giving ourselves to the faithful repetition of our mantra.

The Women at the Cross: Trauma

ᶻᵃ *Near the cross of Jesus stood his mother and his mother's sister, Mary, the wife of Clopas, and Mary of Magdala. Seeing his mother and the disciple he loved standing near her, Jesus said to his mother, "Woman, this is your son." Then to the disciple he said, "This is your mother" (John 19:26–27).* ᶻᵃ

Afraid for their own lives, most of Jesus' disciples fled or viewed his crucifixion from a distance. We know that a small group of women disciples remained close to the cross.

All who have been involved in the suffering and death of one whom they deeply love can identify easily with the feelings of helplessness and loss experienced by these disciples at the cross. We can only speculate about the significance of the women's proximity to Jesus during this terrible ordeal. Did Jesus need those he loved there? Did those who stood with Jesus experience something different because of their physical closeness to him at death?

On Calvary, through Jesus, the power of death was broken. In Jesus, death loses its sting; we are released from the bondage that keeps our human hearts victims of fear. This releasing from bondage addresses all forms of death—whatever it is that keeps the human heart from entrusting itself to the Divine Other.

The traumatic event of Calvary, therefore, can speak to the traumas suffered in our lives. Frequently, the places where we've experienced trauma or terror have coincided with the experience of a loss of innocence. These times of trauma in our lives are often the initiatory experiences of our self-hatred and self-disgust. They identify those events in our personal lives where we begin to perceive ourselves as cut off from our true selves and distant from Divine Intimacy.

Dysfunctional family life, and the chaos and anxiety created by it, may be at the root of our trauma. Perhaps sexual, verbal, emotional, or physical abuse during our growing-up years or our sense of abandonment or betrayal by those we believed loved us were our traumatic experiences. Such experiences can be so heinous that the feelings associated with them cause us to lose contact with the reality of our own goodness, worth, and lovableness. We identify instead with false perceptions of ourselves—our egos— that indict us as evil and unlovable. Consequently, these experiences become for us the place of destructive death—death without the promise of new life.

The women disciples who stood beneath the cross, as well as the disciple John, are the presence of human love during this traumatic event of Jesus' life. They are the witnesses to the pain inflicted on innocence. When we look upon the crucified Jesus, we see what egocentricity looks like. The suffering of Jesus on the cross mirrors back to human history the consequences of identifying with the false self. Jesus, the innocent one, takes on, lets us see its horror, faces into its destructive nature (its death-dealing behavior) and breaks the power it has upon us. The redemptive act of Jesus transmutes egocentricity. Now, the place of Calvary, the place of trauma, becomes the scene of selfless love, of othercenteredness, of innocence restored, of life that goes beyond death.

The traumas of life that keep us distant from the truth of our identity, that create deathlike existences of pretense or overwhelming anxiety and fear need the presence of those who love us to call forth the true self that we have denied or submerged because of traumas. It is this experience of love, the love of the Divine Other and our companions along the way who stay close, that enables and facilitates our naming and facing into in faith the places of destructive death in our lives. It is then that we are freed from the memories and feelings that keep us captives of our ego and its fears.

Each time we enter our prayer of Christian meditation, we turn toward the Divine Other and thereby identify with Truth—with Reality. We are discovered in the Reality who is God, and in this Truth, the reality of ourselves is known—our true selves. As we are freed of egocentricity, we are re-membered to our original innocence and know again that we are loved, whole, and good.

Let us enter our prayer, trusting in the love and power of the Divine Other to draw us into the place of truth.

Pentecost:
A New Consciousness for the
Women and Men Disciples

🔊 . . . *but you will receive power when the Holy Spirit comes on you, and then you will be my witnesses not only in Jerusalem but throughout Judaea and Samaria, and indeed to the ends of the earth. . . .*

So from the Mount of Olives, as it is called, they went back to Jerusalem, a short distance away, no more than a sabbath walk; and when they reached the city they went to the upper room where they were staying; there were Peter and John, James and Andrew, Philip and Thomas, Bartholomew and Matthew, James son of Alphaeus and Simon the Zealot, and Jude son of James. All these joined in continuous prayer, together with several women, including Mary the mother of Jesus, and with his brothers (Acts 1:8, 12–14). 🔊

The veil separating human consciousness from a more complete experience and understanding of God's revelation in Christ is drawn back at the Pentecost experience. Through the power and presence of God's Spirit, those who had waited in the upper room are awakened into new consciousness. The full impact of the salvation brought about in Christ is now realized in these disciples. Empowered in the Spirit, the disciples become witnesses to the life, death, and resurrection of Jesus because now they experience not only faith *in* Jesus, but the faith *of* Jesus. In this reality of faith, the boundaries that separate people dissolve, and the unity realized in Christ becomes the experience of these women and men. The universal language spoken by the disciples reflects this reality and anticipates their understanding of the universal mission of the Church.

Before the Pentecost event, the disciples were filled with fear. As followers of Christ, they were susceptible to his same destiny— persecution and death. The releasing of God's Spirit enables them to transcend their fear and move beyond the confines of their own limitations.

The coalescing of the Christ event with human history is portrayed in the Pentecost experience. Pentecost makes visible to us what has been accomplished in Christ and reminds us of the abiding presence of God's own Spirit in the lives of all women and men. In the disciples present at the Pentecost event, we see women and men set loose, no longer the captives of their fear, but free to respond to the Divine Other in love and service. We know through these women and men disciples the possibility now open to human consciousness.

The mystical truth expressed in the Pentecost event is human consciousness no longer experiencing itself limited by finite boundaries but caught up into Divine Life. This experience of unveiled contact with Divine Love is the realization of oneness— oneness with the Divine Other, with all others, and with oneself.

What is confirmed in the Pentecost experience is the mutuality of love that exists between Creator and creature. We are not left alone and helpless in our desire to be realized in Divine Love. The same Spirit present to Jesus in his life, death, and resurrection dwells in us and will lead us through our life, death, and resurrection.

The Pentecost event for the disciples is an experience of God unmediated by images. Christian meditation is a discipline that aligns our consciousness with the consciousness of the God within us. It calls us, through the use of the mantra, beyond imagination toward the experience of pure prayer—prayer unmediated by images and self-preoccupation. Each time we practice our prayer of Christian meditation, we are awake to the reality of the Pentecost event that is impinging on human consciousness.

Let us now, in simplicity and love, enter our prayer.

The Song of Songs: Wisdom

We find as we read Wisdom literature that its writers were specifically concerned with life's meaning and human experience. Throughout these writings, wisdom is extolled, concretized, and presented as the way of life worth total commitment.

In Proverbs we read: "Better gain wisdom than gold" (16:16).

The search for lasting value is summed up by the author in Ecclesiastes 1:1: "Vanity of vanities! All is vanity."

Wisdom, in the book of Wisdom, is represented as something to be sought after and worthy of sacrifice: "I entreated, and the spirit of Wisdom came to me" (7:7).

In the Wisdom tradition that is part of sacred scripture, more seems to be represented than humanity's attempt to define itself and define its relationship to God. Each book tries to convey what wisdom is like. In the Song of Songs, we find that Wisdom is more than a way of perceiving life, more than a set of principles and beliefs. Wisdom in the Song of Songs is the *experience* of union and completion expressed in the metaphor of the lovers.

As the metaphor for human longing finding completion, the Song re-members us to our fundamental identity. In the Song of Songs, we find the destiny of human life realized in the experience of love.

Our commitment to the prayer of Christian meditation is the pathway to the experience of oneness. The profound delight and joy expressed in the metaphor of the lovers is the result of realizing union, oneness, wholeness, and integrity. It is the experience of Wisdom.

Our commitment to the prayer of Christian meditation is a way to realizing completeness in the Divine Other. The experience of oneness and unity portrayed in this metaphor reflects the ultimate destiny of the human heart as it penetrates the layers of illusion that keep it separated from its ultimate reality—the self known and found in intimate relationship with the Divine Other.

Let us now enter our prayer knowing that we shall be discovered in Love.

Inside Forgiveness

succulent
sweet
this wedding feast
known love
—and more
—an open door
to the unhallwayed
heart of God

led
fed
into forgiveness
savoring
tasting
the deliciousness
of mercy's love
and love of mercy

unrestrained
unsyllabled
joy
becomes the din
within
the chamber
of our hearts
and fills
spills
into being
singing
adoramus te
benedicimus te
glorificamus te

To my friends Kathy McKinney,
Marge Gaughan, and Gypsy da Silva
who helped to prepare this
manuscript for publication
and to the Maryknoll Society who
generously gave me the sabbatical
time for writing and reflection
—to them and for them—
my loving gratitude.